THE COMPLETE BOOK OF
FUNERAL PLANNING

READINGS
❈ & MUSIC ❈

THE COMPLETE BOOK OF
FUNERAL PLANNING
READINGS
& MUSIC

How to plan and organise the funeral
your loved ones would most appreciate

RACHEL JOHNSTONE-BURT, ALISON GIBBS
AND REV. JOHN WYNBURNE

foulsham
LONDON • NEW YORK • TORONTO • SYDNEY

foulsham

The Publishing House, Bennetts Close, Cippenham,
Slough, Berkshire, SL1 5AP, England

Foulsham books can be found in all good bookshops and direct
from www.foulsham.com

ISBN 0-572-03058-4

Printed in Great Britain by Creative Print and Design (Wales), Ebbw Vale

CONTENTS

INTRODUCTION

While it is a topic that we so often try to avoid, death is something we all have to face, and it affects not only one individual but everyone connected with them.

This book is designed to help you in many ways whenever you have to cope with the difficult and emotional subject of funeral planning. It is designed as a comprehensive guide, so it's unlikely that you would ever need all the information you will find here at one time. However, when you have identified your specific needs, you will find straightforward, step-by-step information, support and guidance that will help you cope on both a practical and an emotional level.

If you want to make a will, make financial arrangements or plan your own funeral, it will help you to:
- write your will and choose an executor
- consider how to organise your finances to maximise the benefits and minimise any problems for your loved ones
- organise your personal possessions so they are gifted to those people you would most like to receive them
- decide whether you would like your organs to be available for donation when you die
- plan a funeral that will ensure you are remembered in the way you would most like

If you have to cope with the death of a loved one, it will help you to:
- understand the official processes you will have to navigate
- ensure that the practical issues can be dealt with as simply and efficiently as possible

- understand the process of grieving and the importance of allowing yourself time to move through that process towards healing

If you are planning a funeral, it will help you to:
- create an occasion that truly represents the wishes of your loved one and helps everyone affected by the loss to celebrate his or her life and find consolation in the ritual
- choose appropriate readings
- select suitable music to fit the mood you wish you create

There is a useful section that gives sources of further advice and information on a variety of subjects (see Useful Addresses, pages 335–41).

Most of us need and appreciate help in coping with death. Whether it is in anticipation of an imminent death or planning for a funeral further into the future, having resources at our disposal can be a great help. There are decisions that have to be made and certain things that have to be done. However, it is not easy to deal with the many issues that surround a death and a funeral, especially if we are feeling overwhelmed with grief. Looking ahead to the end of one's own life can also be a challenge on many levels.

There are, moreover, few endings that are not accompanied by some sense of loss and sadness; even ceremonies that are a celebration of a life are often still tinged with sorrow. Likewise, when death is expected and feels like a 'merciful release', especially when somebody has been suffering, grief and sadness are usually mixed with a sense of thanksgiving as we look back.

When we confront death, in either the past, the present or the future, we will almost certainly value emotional support from others, which may come from family and friends, the local community or a caring organisation. It is also helpful to have at our disposal practical information so that, when arranging the final farewell for our loved ones or for ourselves, we plan or offer the very best. It is our hope that this book will provide the resources to do that.

Death and sadness go hand in hand. But death is a natural and inevitable part of the circle of life and one that we will all have to cope with at some time. Bringing it into the open, showing how the official systems work and how they can be implemented, and feeling able to find appropriate ways in which to display our emotions can be a vital part of the healing process.

PART 1
PLANNING YOUR
OWN FUNERAL

YOUR WILL AND FINANCES

One only has to think for a moment about the tragic events of 7 July 2005 in London, 9/11 in the United States or witness the brutality of a motorway pile-up to realise how fragile life is: what if it were you in one of those cars, for example?

One of the many ways in which you can take charge of your destiny is quite simple: you can make a will. This one act will ensure that your assets go where you want them to go and that your loved ones are taken care of after your death.

Almost a third of the population in Britain dies intestate – that is to say they did not make a will before they died. Perhaps they assumed that it would not matter and that their families would automatically get their property, but this is not necessarily the case.

Of course, you may have other reasons for deciding you should make a will. You may have lost a close relative or friend recently; you may have become ill yourself. In any case, facing and then taking control of the inevitable is not only empowering but may also enable you to see death in a more positive light.

Why Should I Make a Will?

A will is a legal document in which we state our final wishes as to the distribution of our property and assets after death.

If you die intestate, your property and possessions will be distributed in a predetermined way according to the intestacy rules in operation at the time, once all the relevant costs have been settled. While this system aims to be reasonably fair, it will not necessarily leave your spouse and dependants better off – rather the opposite might be true if the value of your estate adds up to more than the inheritance tax threshold (see page 28). In addition, the process may take more time and be more complex than it would be if you had made a will.

Even if your affairs are straightforward, it is always in your interests to make a will in which you specify how you want your estate to be distributed. It is particularly important if your financial affairs are complicated, as your will can make the process much simpler. It is also important if you have remarried or have a complex family structure. For example, if you are a man with children from a first marriage and have then remarried and die intestate, your second wife will inherit all your goods, and your children from your first marriage may get nothing. You may also wish to specify exactly how your possessions should be shared. For example, you might want your spouse to inherit your property but your children to benefit from some of your investments. If you want this to happen, then you must say so.

Intestacy Rules
In the absence of a will, for a family with children the intestacy rules provide for the surviving spouse:
- a statutory legacy (see page 14)
- the personal chattels
- a life interest in one half of the residue of the estate

Any children are entitled to the other half of the residue once they reach the age of 18. Children of the deceased are defined as being:
- legitimate children
- illegitimate children
- adopted children

Step-children are not regarded as children of the deceased under intestacy rules.

If there are no children, the statutory legacy for the surviving spouse is increased.

A spouse, that is the person to whom the deceased was married even if they were separated or estranged, can nevertheless inherit a share of the estate under intestacy rules.

A divorced husband or wife cannot inherit under intestacy rules.

2005–6 intestacy rates
* statutory legacy to a spouse with children is £125,000
* statutory legacy to a spouse with no children is
   £200,000

Other circumstances lead to different allocations. If you die
without a spouse or children, then the legal rights to your
property would go, in order, to:
● your parents
● your brothers and sisters
● your half-brothers and half-sisters
● your grandparents

The authorities that deal with these matters will work
through any remaining family in order. So, after exhausting
the primary family, any aunts, uncles, cousins etc. may claim
the allowance, provided there are no closer living relatives. If,
after the award has been made to, say, a cousin, a long-lost son
of the deceased turns up, then the cousin would probably have
to forfeit the inheritance.

If there are no surviving relatives, the estate will pass to the
Crown. This alone is an excellent reason for making a will
now, as even if you do not have immediate family, you could
choose to leave everything to a friend, a neighbour or perhaps a
charity that is close to your heart.

Notes for those co-habiting
A partner with whom you are living but are not married to has
no rights whatsoever under existing legislation, which is why it
is even more important if you are unmarried but co-habiting to
ensure that you have made proper provision for your partner.

With regard to home ownership, if you are not married
then your partner will be treated less favourably after your
death. If your home is not jointly owned, your partner will not

be able to claim any share in it without proof that he or she contributed to its acquisition and improvement.

If you are co-habiting in a rented property, you must check with your landlord to make sure that he or she is happy for your partner to continue living in the property and is prepared to take on your partner as the new tenant. Rights of succession are granted to protect tenants under the Rent Act 1977. These rights are granted to:

- your spouse
- your partner with whom you are living as man and wife, or with whom you are living in a long-standing same-sex relationship
- a member of your family who has lived with you for at least two years before your death

The obvious choice in these cases is to see a solicitor, but if you are conscious of the cost, visit your local Citizens Advice Bureau for help and advice beforehand.

Gay and Lesbian Concerns

From December 2005, the Civil Partnership Act will protect gay and lesbian partnerships in law. If you decide to sign up to the register, you will then receive equal rights with married couples on pensions and inheritance tax. Nevertheless you should always make a will to ensure that your partner is the beneficiary of your assets. (See also pages 34 and 138-9.)

If you and your gay partner are co-habiting in a council house, and you are the tenant, the tenancy rights may not necessarily be inherited by your partner. Check with your local authority to see what its rules are so that you can make sure your partner is protected in the event of your death. Usually there will be no problem whatsoever, particularly if you have been co-habiting for more than two years, but do check anyway. You should be fully protected under the Rent Act 1977.

How Do I Make a Will?

A large number of us assume that simply writing out on a sheet of paper what we want to do with our assets is enough, and that this piece of paper is therefore a legal and binding document. This is not always the case. The truth is that, unless a will has been written and witnessed in a particular way, it could, after your death, be open to misinterpretation and therefore will not necessarily be seen as valid in the eyes of the law. To be certain that your last wishes are properly observed, it is worth finding out all you can about the various options that are available to you so that you can make an informed decision as to how you should proceed.

The options that are available when it comes to making and writing a will are to:

- use a DIY kit or online service
- use a bank or building society will-writing service
- go to a solicitor

DIY Kits

Of course, it is possible to write your own will, and this is the cheapest option. There are several very affordable DIY versions available in good stationer's shops. The best feature a CD-Rom that takes you through the correct procedures, an explanatory leaflet, a checklist, a will form, and a few other useful bits and pieces. These kits are produced by solicitors, so this is a safe and cheap way of making sure your estate is divided up in the way you wish while at the same time observing the legalities.

There are also online will-making services, for example at www.thewillsite.co.uk and www.easierwills.co.uk, where you can make a will for a small fee.

In short, DIY wills and online will services represent excellent value but they must be written and witnessed in a certain way, otherwise they are not valid, so do be careful and take advice if necessary.

Bank and Building Society Services

Some of the high street banks offer a will-making service, but these should be approached with a degree of caution as some may charge quite a high premium in administration costs after your death. If your bank offers a will-writing service and you wish to take advantage of it, do be sure to read the small print in the terms and conditions leaflet, which should be provided with any of their information packs.

Solicitors

One of the safest options is to ask a solicitor to write your will for you. A solicitor who specialises in will-writing will be well versed in the legal language required and will be able to guide you through the various procedures. As well as general solicitors, many legal companies specialise in this service.

If your affairs are relatively simple, this will involve nothing more than one or two meetings, and most companies offer a fixed-fee service that is only slightly more expensive than an online service. Obviously, such costs will be higher if your affairs are complex – but the more complicated they are, the more important it is that you have a sound will.

Approximate costs for will-writing services
* DIY kits: £15–20
* online services: £40 for a single person and £60 for a joint application
* bank and building society: from about £60
* solicitor: from about £60

As part of his or her fee, a solicitor will also store your will for you and act as executor or joint executor on the document (see pages 21–2 and 23–4), so you can be assured of professional advice at the time of your death.

If you think your assets might be worth more than the current inheritance tax threshold (see page 28), then you should consider using a solicitor. Many of us in the UK own a property, and you need only to look at the average price for a house, coupled with any other assets you may have, to realise that this could push your allowance over the inheritance tax threshold. While the tax threshold tends to increase slightly year on year, in line with inflation and other economic factors, it still makes sense to consider visiting a solicitor for advice if nothing else. He or she will be able to tell you how inheritance tax can affect your estate, what your family's rights are, and approximately what the tax burden on your family will be after you die.

If there is anything remotely complicated about your assets, then you should always consult a solicitor; if, for example:

- you own any property overseas
- you are not a British citizen
- your permanent home is not in the UK
- you have financial dependants who might wish to make a claim on your estate after your death
- you own all or part of a business

Without the help of an expert, there is a chance you could make a serious error that could cost your family dear after your death, at a time when they will be coping with the grief of your loss and are least able to focus on financial complexities.

Many of us do own a little property and, however small those assets may be, if we really care about what happens to our families after our deaths, it is not logical to leave everything to the Government to decide what should be done with your money and possessions, and perhaps have it end up going to the Crown. Your family certainly won't be looked after in the same way by the Government as they will be if you have the foresight to spend a little time and money in making a will.

If you do not have a solicitor and would like to consult with one, you can either look in your local Yellow Pages or telephone The Law Society (see Useful Addresses, page 338) for a list of solicitors in your area.

It should be pointed out that using a solicitor to make your will is probably the most sensible thing to do. It may be more expensive than any of the DIY options, but at least you can be certain that your wishes will be carried out to the letter.

Listing Your Assets and Liabilities

Before you visit a solicitor or any other organisation for advice, sit down and write a list of your assets and liabilities as, without this information, your adviser will be unable to assess properly the kind of assistance you might need. You should include:

- All your possessions, including your car and the contents of the garage.
- Bank and building society accounts.
- Credit and store cards.
- Debts.
- If you own a house, the current value of your house.
- If you have a mortgage, the details of the value of your mortgage, the lender and the length of time the mortgage has to run.
- If you rent a council house, the details of the contract. Can the tenancy be transferred to your spouse or partner? Or, if your children live with you, can the tenancy be transferred to one of them? Check with your local council and find out. A solicitor will be able to clarify whether or not you need to specify this in your will.
- Life insurance policies. With whom do you have policies and what is their total value?
- The value of your pension plan and the company name.
- Any other assets you may have: perhaps you have a timeshare apartment or some stocks and shares. Include everything in your list.
- The names and dates of birth of your children and the people you have selected as their guardians (see page 21).

- The name and address of the person you have chosen to act as your executor (see pages 21–2).
- Any specific bequests you would like to make. For example, you may want a particular painting to be given to your son, or your jewellery to your daughter.

Use this list to ask yourself how you would like your assets to be distributed after your death. You may have no surviving family and would like to leave what you have to a charity you favour or perhaps you may wish friends to benefit instead.

Division of Your Personal Possessions

It would be nice to think that your heirs might be able to do this on their own but, if in doubt, play it safe. It might be a good idea to allocate your personal possessions by name, thus ensuring that your heirs suffer no additional heartache and pain. Where emotions are running high in the first place, and they are sure to be after your death, shock and grief can make any of us behave irrationally or even out of character.

If you have promised one person a particular piece of furniture or jewellery, make sure this is stated. It will help avoid any friction and upset.

If you have no heirs and there is no one you feel you want to name as heir, do make a will anyway, preferably in favour of a charity, or a similar organisation where your money can make a difference. Your gift will be received with real gratitude. Remember, if you do not make a will, the Crown may get your entire estate.

If you have already made a will, perhaps in favour of your spouse or partner or children, you may decide later that you'd like to make a few additions. Perhaps you'd like to settle a little bit of cash on a grandchild or leave a small token to a new friend. Instead of rewriting your entire will, you can simply add these on to your existing will in the form of a codicil. This must be written in the right way, duly witnessed and signed for validity.

Minors

If you are thinking of making a will, for whatever reason, and you have young children, you should think about the appointment of a guardian should both you and your partner die. A guardian can also be appointed if one of you dies, to help the surviving parent.

Both parents have the right to appoint a guardian if they are, or were, married to each other. The mother has the automatic right to appoint a guardian, whereas the father can appoint a guardian only if:

- he was married to the mother at the time of the child's/children's birth, or
- he was given parental responsibility for the child/children by a court order, or
- he entered into a parental responsibility agreement with the child's/children's mother

Where the father is married to the mother, then the guardian he appoints will act jointly with the mother after his death, unless he specifies that the guardian is to step in only after the deaths of both parents.

If your estate is not worth a huge amount and you feel that going to a solicitor is an unnecessary expense, you can informally appoint a guardian for your child. This appointment must be in writing, and it must be dated and signed. There are no legal requirements for witnesses to this, but it would be wise just in case to have at least one. Obviously, you must ask the person you wish to appoint beforehand to ensure he or she is willing to undertake this responsibility.

Choosing an Executor

The executor is the person who will oversee the distribution of your assets in accordance with the instructions you leave in your will.

Most people opt for either their spouse/partner, an adult child, a close relative such as a brother or sister, or a trusted friend. It might be an advantage if you have the option to choose someone with financial expertise as executor though this is by no means essential. Some people choose to ask their solicitor to perform this duty.

An independent executor can be appointed but will have to be paid for his or her services. It might be wise to appoint an independent person if you suspect that your will may be challenged or if you feel your family may squabble after your death. It can happen, however specific you might have been in your will, so it is something that should be considered for the sake of lasting peace in the family.

A popular choice is to appoint a member of the family and your solicitor to act as co-executors as this can also help avoid potential pitfalls.

Don't forget to ask each of these nominated people if they mind acting as your executor – and do warn them that sometimes an estate can take some time to wind up, and that their responsibilities to it may drag on for longer than they might have anticipated.

Finally, don't forget that you should choose an executor whom you expect to survive you.

What Happens Next?

Once you have accumulated the data, you can then either think about writing your will yourself or search for a reputable solicitor. He or she, armed with the information you have provided, will be able to assess the best way of dealing with your estate, will be able to provide you with expert guidance, and may even be able to save you and your family money. For further information, call The Law Society (see Useful Addresses, page 338) or, if you live in Scotland, you can telephone The Scottish Executive Civil Law Division (see Useful Addresses, page 340).

The solicitor will then draw up your will to include all the information you have provided. If there are any queries, obviously he or she will resolve these with you during that process.

Once this has been done, the document will not be recognised as being valid until it has been signed by you and by two independent witnesses. The rules here are that neither the witnesses nor any of their relations should be people who will benefit from your will. If you have opted for a DIY will, please do remember this point as your will could be rendered invalid if it is not properly witnessed. If you are using one, your solicitor and a member of his or her staff will be able to witness the will.

If you have a will drawn up by a solicitor and you then unfortunately die before you have had time to sign the will, in a court of law the judge will probably agree that the will is administered according to your wishes. If you have made a DIY will, this outcome is less certain, and your family members could find themselves stuck under the intestacy rules (see pages 13–14).

Storing Your Will

Most solicitors will be happy to keep a copy of your will for you and this is a good idea. There is sometimes a small charge for this service but many solicitors do not charge anything at all. If you do decide to keep your will at home, make sure it is in a safe place. Wherever you keep it, you should make sure that at least your executor knows where your will is stored. In the immediate aftermath of your death, this document must be easily accessible so that your executor can begin the process of sorting out your estate as soon as possible.

Keep a separate copy of your will at home with a full list of your financial data. The financial data list should include the following information:

- the location of your will and other personal documents
- details of any funeral plan, pre-paid or otherwise, including the name of the company and the policy number

- whether you would prefer burial or cremation, and any other wishes you may have for disposal of your body.
- the details (names and addresses, phone numbers etc.) of your executors, solicitor, accountant, bank manager, stockbroker etc.
- your tax district and reference number
- details of your main assets, bank names and account numbers, building society account names and numbers
- details of mortgage(s) and lender(s)
- details of any liabilities – debts etc.
- details of all credit and store cards, including account numbers, plus any outstanding amounts owed
- pension and insurance arrangements
- any inheritance tax history – e.g. information about any gifts received within the previous seven years

Keeping Your Will Up to Date

Once you have made a will and have stored it safely – either with your solicitor or at home – you will need to review its contents whenever there are any major changes in your financial and family circumstances. The list of financial data will also need updating at regular intervals.

If you are young and in good health, you will not need to revisit your will more than once every five years, unless of course your circumstances alter. You may have another child, for example and wish to include him or her in your will. If there are any big changes then you should think about having a new will drawn up, but for small alterations you can add what are known as 'codicils' – little extra clauses, tacked on to the end of an existing will. They will also need to be signed and witnessed in the normal way otherwise they will be invalid.

Keeping the information as current as possible will help your estate to be expedited smoothly. It is easy to update your information if you store it on a computer database, but do remember to keep a back-up copy.

Revising Your Will

It is important that you update your will to allow for changes in your own or your family circumstances. Revising your will, however, is not something to be done on impulse but should be done with careful thought and consideration. For example, if you wish to make provision for a new partner, you should consider fully the consequences on other members of the family. You may wish to inform the parties involved so that they know and understand why you have made the alterations. While it is recognised that many families today are affected by marital breakdowns and there are many reconstituted or 'blended' families, remember to be kind to those connected to you by kinship. Although it may never have been expressed, it is surprising how much you may have mattered to those with whom your recent association has been impaired or lost.

Although a rarity, there are circumstances in which you could run the risk of your will subsequently being challenged on the grounds that you were not of 'sound mind' when you made the changes. If you feel there are genuine reasons that this could happen, it is possible to obtain a certificate from a doctor affirming that your state of mind is sound.

It is best not to rely on verbal promises you make to family, friends or carers as there will be no proof that such promises were made and the executor is legally bound to honour the terms of the written will. The beneficiaries may be aware of a verbal promise but there is no compulsion for them to be honoured, so it is always best to put all your wishes in writing in your will. Again, make sure that each change and addition is signed and witnessed to ensure its validity.

Revoking Your Will

Occasionally certain events may make you wish to revoke your will either because you have made a later will or you want to destroy the existing one.

In certain circumstances the law regards a will as having been automatically revoked. Those circumstances are as follows:

- **By destruction.** Occasionally a testator (the person who makes the will) may destroy a will for his or her own reasons. Outright physical destruction such as burning the will or tearing it up clearly indicates revocation. A line drawn through a page or part of a page is not sufficient to revoke the will. If the will can still be clearly read and the signatures are visible, then it is still deemed to be valid because it is not clear whether a line through text means it should be revoked – it could be just a slip of a pen.

- **By divorce.** If the testator divorces after the will has been made, then that will is partially revoked; the will remains valid but any bequests to the former spouse are automatically deleted. However, separation without divorce has no effect on the will and it remains valid.

- **By marriage.** If a person makes a will in favour of a nephew, for example, and then afterwards he or she marries, the pre-existing will is revoked.

- **By a later will or codicil.** Usually later wills will state that any former wills are no longer valid. However, if a later will does not expressly revoke all former wills and your executor is left confused by apparently conflicting last wishes, the executor can make a judgement based on implication. The last (that is, the latest) 'Last Will and Testament' is usually assumed to be the valid one. If the two wills are consistent with each other then they can both be administered. For example, a later will may add a few bequests, perhaps to carers who have made the last few months of the person's life more comfortable.

Inheritance Tax

This section can be a guide only as it concerns a very complex area of financial management. Most of the big high street banks operate advisory services for these matters and will be able to refer you to a financial adviser who will be able to help you.

The inheritance tax threshold is fixed annually and is the amount you are allowed to inherit tax-free. The total value of an estate, if it does not exceed this figure, will not attract any tax; however anything over this amount will be taxed. There are some exemptions and reliefs, and married partners of those who have died do not pay inheritance tax. However, any other relatives who might be due to inherit assets will have to pay inheritance tax.

What Does a Person's Estate Include?

Excepting any money or property not covered by any exemption (see Inheritance Tax Exemptions and Reliefs, below), your estate includes:

- the total value of everything owned in your name, less bills, funeral expenses and mortgages owing at the time of death
- the share of anything jointly owned, less your share of joint bills and mortgages owing at the time of death
- the capital value of trust funds from which you have received some benefit; for example, income received as a 'life tenant' under the trust or if you had the right to live in a house
- gifts of money or property made less than seven years before death (see Potentially Exempt Transfers, pages 29–30)

In addition, sometimes property that you have given away may be treated as part of the estate for inheritance tax purposes; if you gave a house to another member of the family but continued to live in it, then this will be dealt with under the gifts with reservations rules (see page 29).

Inheritance Tax Exemptions and Reliefs

There are only a few exceptions to inheritance tax liability. There will be no tax on:

- the assets and property left to your spouse, provided he or she resides in the UK
- assets and property left to charity

- assets and property left to the heirs of a member of the armed forces killed in action

---

Inheritance tax and non-UK residence
* if your spouse lives outside the UK, there will be inheritance tax liability on assets and property he or she inherits with a value exceeding the 2005–2006 exemption figure of £55,000

There are also tax reliefs, though not complete exemption, that reduce the value of qualifying property, for example business assets and farmland.

For further information see leaflet HT17, which is available from your local tax office.

How inheritance tax is calculated
In the tax year 2005–6, the inheritance tax threshold is £275,000. (Recent Land Registry figures suggest that if the inheritance tax threshold had increased in line with property prices, then it would now stand at £513,850!) On estates that are valued at up to or less than £5,000, there are no charges to pay.

If your estate is valued at up to or less than the current inheritance tax threshold, your heirs are not liable for any tax but they will have to pay a probate fee, currently £130.

If your estate is valued at more than the threshold, you pay 40 per cent on the remaining monies. For example:
* the probate value of your estate = £500,000
* the inheritance tax allowance = £275,000
* leaving £225,000, which is taxable at 40 per cent
* therefore the tax bill will be £90,0000
* leaving your heirs with a total of £410,000

How to Hold on to Your Cash and Keep it in the Family

The Inland Revenue takes strenuous action to crack down on inheritance tax avoidance, so you should perhaps start thinking about a strategy for protecting your assets in the best interests of your family. With just a little forward planning you can still legitimately avoid some major traps that could leave your family worse off after your death.

The Inland Revenue focuses in particular on arrangements whereby people have given away their assets, usually to their children, while continuing to benefit from those assets. For example, the tax man will be very interested in a situation where parents have made over their home to their offspring yet have continued to live in it. This is no longer a way to avoid inheritance tax.

Gifts and Gifts with Reservations

You can make a number of annual and one-off gifts of money each year to any number of individuals, or on the marriage of a child. You can make gifts of any size providing they are seen to be normal expenditure out of your income.

All gifts to UK charities, political parties and national institutions are free from interhitance tax and, if you live in a heritage property, then that too will be exempt, providing certain criteria are met.

A gift with reservations is a term coined to describe the gift of property or other assets to someone else while continuing to enjoy the benefits of them. With effect from April 2005, there is now an income tax charge on the benefit gained from using them. How these will be calculated depends on the value of the assets. For further information, contact your local Inland Revenue office.

Potentially Exempt Transfers

Assets given away during your lifetime are also known as potentially exempt transfers. This means that you must survive for seven years after the gift in order for the beneficiaries of your gift to be able to avoid inheritance tax. If you should die within the seven-year time frame, then a sliding scale tax will be applied. This relief applies only to gifts that fall outside the inheritance tax allowance.

Insurance can be arranged to cover any liability during this seven-year period, though policies should be written in trust so that the proceeds will not be regarded as part of your estate and can be paid immediately to your family after your death.

Gifts and potentially exempt transfers
You can give £250 annually to any number of individuals.

If you have given a gift of money or property of a higher value to someone within seven years of death and it falls outside the inheritance tax allowance, there are potential liabilities, though there is still some advantage to be gained provided the gift was made three years before death. Gifts given:

* 6–7 years before death are taxed at 20 per cent of the inheritance tax rate
* 5–6 years before death are taxed at 40 per cent of the inheritance tax rate
* 4–5 years before death are taxed at 60 per cent of the inheritance tax rate
* 3–4 years before death are taxed at 80 per cent of the inheritance tax rate
* less than 3 years before death are taxed at the full inheritance tax rate

---

Exemptions for Married Partners
Your spouse, if still alive at the time of your death, will automatically inherit your estate without having to pay any inheritance tax, provided he or she resides in the UK.

If you and your husband or wife have several children and a large percentage of your estate is liquid, that is, easily realised; you can make simple tax savings by bequeathing the equivalent inheritance tax threshold sum to your children, payable when one of you dies, while the residue of your estate will pass, tax-free, to the surviving spouse. When the surviving spouse dies, the children will inherit the remaining estate, and a second phase of the tax-free allowance. By using the tax-exempt allowance twice over you could be saving your heirs a considerable amount of money.

Business and Agricultural Reliefs
There are some generous reliefs available for business and agricultural properties, which in some cases can mean that there will be no inheritance tax liability at all.

Back-to-back Schemes
These involve buying a purchased life annuity, which will pay a higher income than a pension annuity. You can then use the income to pay regular premiums for a term or whole of life assurance policy, which should be written in trust to pay your heirs' tax bill. The cost of the annuity and the life assurance premiums will reduce the value of your estate for tax purposes.

Equity Release Schemes
Lifetime mortgages and reversion schemes reduce the value of your estate immediately. With a home-reversion scheme, the owner sells their home, or a percentage of their home, to a plan provider in return for a cash lump sum or a monthly income, or a combination of both. The person can remain in the house rent-free until the last remaining borrower (if a couple) dies or is transferred into long-term care. When the property is sold, the plan provider reclaims their percentage, with the remainder going towards specified beneficiaries. The same percentage of any future rise in the value of the home would also belong to the plan provider.

With a cash-release scheme, the homeowner takes out a fixed-rate, interest-only mortgage on their property and uses the borrowed money to purchase a regular income. There are no monthly repayments to be made as the interest is accumulated over the life of the mortgage. When the borrower dies or is moved into long-term care, the original loan plus accumulated interest is repaid.

Family Trusts

Pre-owned assets tax (POAT) is an annual income tax charge on the benefit of someone living in a property they have sold (that is to say made over to another or exchanged for a nominal sum), without paying full rent. People using equity release schemes are exempt, as are those whose home has an annual rental value below a certain value (see below).

Family trust values
People are exempt whose home has an annual rental value below £5,000 for a sole occupant or £10,000 for a couple.

The Inland Revenue will also exempt those who have sold their property for a consideration other than money or any other readily realisable asset. Tax specialists take this to mean that a property transfer to a child who moves in with a parent to care for him or her will be exempt.

Although the Inland Revenue insists the tax will not be retrospective, it will be retroactive, which means that anyone who has set up a scheme since March 1986 and which falls within the POAT net could be liable to an income tax charge based on the annual market rental value of their property after 6 April 2005.

The POAT net
Someone living in a house valued at £750,000 with an annual rental value of £45,000 will have to pay £18,000 in income tax, assuming they are a higher-rate taxpayer, unless they elect to bring the house into the inheritance tax net. This election must be made by 31 January 2007.

Rental valuations must be carried out at five-yearly intervals.

Will Trusts

For married couples wishing to make use of both their inheritance tax exemptions but whose estate consists principally of the family home, a will trust allows you to arrange your wills so that whoever dies first loans the amount of the inheritance-tax allowance to the surviving spouse, while bequeathing assets equal to the nil-rate band to the children.

The surviving spouse becomes a discretionary beneficiary who inherits all the deceased spouse's assets on the understanding that the designated sum is on loan from the trust. On the death of the surviving spouse, the loan is repaid to the trust and the money is deducted from the value of the estate before inheritance tax. The remaining assets pass to the children net of the inheritance threshold at the time (see page 28).

Loan Trusts

If you wish to receive an income from your assets while retaining a degree of control, a loan trust scheme involves making an interest-free loan to a trust, which invests for capital growth in an investment bond.

Assets held in trust fall outside your estate for inheritance tax purposes so that, if you make a loan to the trust, the trustees, including yourself, make pre-arranged payments of the loan to yourself of 5 per cent per annum, on which higher-rate tax is deferred.

Providing you spend this money as you receive it, this will gradually reduce the value of your estate, while the trust creates capital growth. On your death, the funds accumulated will become part of your estate.

Gay and Lesbian Concerns

The law on inheritance tax has finally been addressed with regard to same-sex partners and, when new legislation comes into force in December 2005, the law will cease to discriminate against those who are gay and lesbian and their partners. They will have the opportunity to have their relationships legally recognised under the Civil Partnerships Act. If they decide to sign up to the partnership register, they will receive equal rights with married couples on financial matters such as pensions and inheritance tax.

LIVING WILLS AND ORGAN DONATION

As more and more amazing medical treatments are available that can alleviate or even cure specific health problems, many of us assume we will live longer than earlier generations ever expected to. Medical advances offer us the opportunity to benefit from organ transplantation, as either a donor or recipient. However, they also raise the question of the quality of life we would wish for if our health deteriorates.

Living Wills

Those of us who might unfortunately go on to develop degenerative illnesses, such as motor neurone disease, can also expect to be kept alive for far longer than we might want or need. With this in mind, there is currently much debate about whether or not we should be making living wills. The *Oxford English Dictionary* defines the term as being 'a written statement of a person's desire not to be kept alive by artificial means in the event of terminal illness or accident'. There is still much reluctance to promote or promulgate living wills since it is a highly controversial and emotional subject.

For those of us who are in good health, the thought of being imprisoned by a condition that inhibits movement and speech and renders us dependent on the goodwill of others may be an appalling prospect. However, what action we might choose to take in those circumstances can vary widely, and it is up to each individual to think carefully about the options, discuss his or her thoughts with those close to them and take appropriate action.

Some people believe that life is precious at any price and that living wills are a licence for legitimate euthanasia, which many may find a repellent concept. *The Diving Bell and the Butterfly*, published in 1997, was written by Jean-Dominique Bauby, who suffered from shut-in syndrome following a stroke, where his mind was intact but he was able to move only his left eyelid. It is well worth reading, not only because it is beautifully written but also because it expresses perfectly how, for some, life is valuable regardless of circumstances. For such people, obviously, a living will is irrelevant.

On the other hand, some people feel that they would prefer not to be kept alive under those circumstances. If you feel strongly that this is your position and you have absolute faith in those who will ultimately be caring for you, then you can write down your wishes so that they are respected by your next of kin. The best way to do this is by adding a codicil to your will.

Although living wills are not legally binding under an Act of Parliament, they should be respected under common law, provided that the person writing the living will:

- was over 18 when the document was written and signed
- was not suffering at the time from any mental distress
- was not unduly influenced by anyone else
- was fully informed about the treatment options at the time
- has not subsequently modified the instructions verbally or in writing

Age Concern (see Useful Addresses, page 335) produces an information sheet with full details on living wills.

Revisit Your Living Will Regularly

If you have made a decision to write a living will asking not to be revived in the event of a progressively debilitating illness, you should check and revise it regularly as improved treatments and new drugs for a multitude of previously incurable diseases are being developed all the time.

Organ Donation

There is currently a huge shortage of donor organs in the UK, and any one of us at any time could find ourselves in a situation where perhaps a close relative or friend, or even ourselves, might need a transplant of some sort. Hearts, lungs, kidneys, livers and eye corneas are among the organs most frequently needed.

It is an important decision to make and should not be undertaken lightly, so taking your time to make an informed decision makes a lot of sense. Because of the nature of the procedure, permission to donate an organ has to be given by the next of kin immediately after a person dies, so it is vital to think in advance about whether or not you might be willing, in the event of your death, to donate your organs to improve the quality of life for another human being or even to save his or her life.

At a time when they may be reeling with shock and distress, it is very difficult for the attending doctors to approach the family and ask them if they might consider a gift of such magnitude. Making this decision in advance will allow your next of kin to express your wishes and avoid any distress he or she may feel at an extraordinarily difficult time if they are not sure that this is what you would have wanted.

Relatives who have given their consent in the face of their grief have later reported how much it helped them through the darkest days, knowing that their loss had given hope and life to others and made the death of their loved one less meaningless. There was also a sense of their loved one living on in others.

If you are willing to be a donor, all you need to do is tell your next of kin and carry a donor card. On the other hand, if, on whatever grounds, you object to having your organs donated, you should make your feelings known to your next of kin.

The Rules for Organ Donation
Any patient will be considered a suitable donor for organ transplant if he or she is:
- under the age of 75
- has been in good health until that time but has died in hospital
- is deemed to be brain dead and is being kept on a life-support system

A patient will not be considered a suitable donor for organ transplant if:
- the death occurred at home
- the death has been reported to the coroner (though with the coroner's permission organs can be removed for donation)

Proposed Opt-out System for Organ Donation
The UK national shortage of donated organs needed for transplant, research and other purposes has reached a crisis level. The desperate need of so many patients waiting for donor kidneys, hearts and livers amongst other organs far outstrips the supply.

The proposal that organs could be donated automatically unless a person has registered an objection has been met with some hostility and at present there are no further plans to pursue this agenda.

Donating Your Body for Medical Research
Another option that you might care to consider is donating your body for medical research.

First of all you should indicate in your will that you would like your body to be donated for medical research purposes, and you should ensure that the executor of your will knows and understands this. He or she should contact HM Inspector of Anatomy (see Useful Addresses, page 338) as soon as possible after your death.

If this is your intention, then you should apply for and complete the necessary forms, and lodge them with your solicitor or next of kin. If you have not done this before you die, then your next of kin will have to do it for you afterwards.

Unfortunately, not all bodies will be accepted for medical research, so it might be wise for you and your family to make some preliminary funeral arrangements for after your death just in case. If the body is accepted, then the medical school in question will arrange for it to be collected. The death should then be registered in the normal way.

Finally, make sure your family members know your wishes. Provided they understand well in advance what you want, and know what to do as soon as you die, they will be able to act promptly. Since there will not be a funeral with burial or cremation, they will probably want to organise a memorial service or a service of thanksgiving.

FUNERAL COSTS

Thinking about making your will may have prompted you to take things one step further and consider your funeral, what you might like and how it will be paid for. This idea may seem, at first, a little morbid, but if you want to minimise the negative impact on your family and ensure that your life is celebrated in the way you would most like, it can actually be a very comforting process.

One of the things that can happen after somebody dies is that the bereaved family and friends find themselves in an emotional no-man's land, groping their way through a morass of shock, grief and uncertainty. They try desperately to remember what the deceased might have wanted, whether or not he or she had strong feelings about burial or cremation. They struggle with the choices on offer which, though relatively few, are nevertheless numerous enough to cause confusion.

Having an established plan will help to smooth the process of transition for them in an emotional sense, and so help them to avoid this extra stress. It will also help them in a practical way because decisions will be straightforward. The financial impact will also be positive as, if you have taken out a pre-paid funeral plan, it will help immeasurably with expenses; your accounts will have been frozen almost straight away after your death and your spouse or partner could be left without access to funds.

Funeral Expenses

One of the first things to think about is how the funeral should be funded.

Most people are on a budget and it is important to factor in the costs when discussing these issues. Unfortunately, everything to do with funerals has a price tag attached, so do keep this in mind. If your budget is slim, asking your family to make sure you are buried in a sumptuous casket might mean that you could bankrupt your estate before probate has even been granted. Funeral costs do vary regionally, and cremation is less expensive, but all the elements of the funeral have to be funded so do take this into account when you are making your plans.

Average funeral costs
* funeral with burial £2,500
* funeral with cremation £1,700

The Office of Fair Trading has launched online advice for those who are arranging a funeral and it is worth consulting the site to make sure your family will be getting a fair deal. See www.oft.gov.uk. Useful information and news is also available at www.uk-funerals.co.uk.

Life Insurance

You may think that any life cover you have will take care of funeral expenses, but unfortunately this is not always the case. Life insurance is usually only for a fixed term. If you die within the term of the policy, then the company will pay out the money, which will indeed cover funeral expenses and all the other incidentals your family will need while your estate is being sorted out. If you survive the term of the policy, however, you (and your family) will get nothing. There are other forms of life cover, which do cover funeral expenses, but these policies tend to be more expensive.

Financial Planning

You can make provision for your funeral by:

- investing a sum of money in a building society, ISA or other savings scheme
- joining one of the societies that pay the costs of a funeral on death
- taking out an insurance policy that will pay for your funeral
- taking out a co-operative funeral bond
- taking out a pre-paid funeral plan

Savings Accounts and ISAs

Any investment will carry with it some risk, so you may feel in the end that it would be more prudent to put some money aside in a building society account. You can add to it as and when you please and it will accumulate a small amount of interest. Alternatively there are ISAs and similar safe investment schemes, which will also help offset the costs of your funeral. Cash Mini ISAs are instant access savings accounts, free from income tax, with quite a good rate of interest (paid monthly) and no hidden charges. There is a limit on the amount you can save each year, but the annual amount is currently more than the average cost of a funeral so that should not be a problem. The advantages of these accounts are that they are immediately accessible so can be used for purposes other than funeral expenses.

Friendly Societies

There are a number of friendly societies currently operating funeral plans that pay out a lump sum when death occurs. These are worth investigating as they do seem to provide excellent value for money. The Association of Friendly Societies (see page 335) is a good source of information.

Insurance Policies

If you have any insurance policies of any kind – life, car, home or contents – then perhaps you can approach your own insurance company for advice. Some insurance companies offer a policy specifically aimed at the 50–80 age group, which is designed to provide life cover and funeral expenses up to a substantial maximum sum. The monthly premiums start at a fairly modest level but you can pay in at different levels on a monthly basis. If you decide to cancel your policy, however, while you would get some of your money back, you would not get the whole sum returned and, if you cancel in the early years of your policy, you might get nothing back at all. On the plus side, some schemes do not require medicals or other health investigations, and guarantee acceptance of all applicants, regardless of their state of health.

If your insurance company does not provide funeral cover, it may be able to provide information on a sister company that does. Alternatively you could ask your financial adviser.

It is also very important to ensure that life insurance policies are written in trust for the benefit of named relatives so that any payments do not form part of your own estate for tax purposes.

Funeral Bonds
You can also enquire at your local funeral directors, many of whom now run their own private insurance schemes and/or you can pick up a leaflet with details of the funeral bond available from most large co-operative stores.

Pre-paid Funeral Plans
Pre-paid funeral plans have become increasingly popular in the past few years. They are usually sold as being tomorrow's funeral at today's prices, and indeed most of them do offer very good value for money – over 300,000 funerals are paid for in the UK in this way each year.

The companies that underwrite these schemes run them in much the same way as any other form of insurance. You pay your premiums, they invest your money, and in return your family is guaranteed a decent funeral for you with all costs covered. Some schemes will include a caveat – so, for example, if your funeral comes at a time when the costs of burial or cremation have risen above the rate of inflation, then your family may have to pay extra charges. The best advice therefore is always to read the small print, so you can be sure you know what you are entitled to.

Most of the schemes offer varying levels of pre-paid funeral: basic, standard and superior or premium.

- The basic scheme consists of a simple funeral service, coffin, cremation and the undertaker's costs. Burial under this particular scheme will cost a little more, so you may have to pay a slightly higher premium if you do not want to be cremated.

- The standard service is the same as above but with a better-quality coffin, cars and some flowers and includes the costs of burial or cremation.

- The superior or premium funeral scheme is as above but with all the trimmings, including a solid wood coffin, cars, flowers, and burial or cremation plus a number of other services. These will vary depending on your choice of funeral director.

Some pre-paid funeral schemes allow you to pick and choose between the options and you are able to create your own funeral from what is on offer at a specially tailored price.

To make sure that the scheme you have opted for is bona fide, you can check with the Office of Fair Trading (see Useful Addresses, page 339), which will be able to tell you whether or not the proceeds from your plan are going to be safely invested with a recognised body. All pre-paid funeral plan providers should be regulated by the Financial Services Authority.

Once you have chosen your pre-paid plan you can either pay into the scheme with a lump sum or you can pay in instalments. It should be noted that, if you are paying in instalments and you die before you have completed your payments, your executor(s) will have to pay the insurance company the rest of the amount you would have paid to the end of the policy term, less the interest on that sum.

PLANNING YOUR
OWN FUNERAL

The natural progression from making a will to setting money
aside for your funeral might be to put a little thought into what
kind of occasion you want your funeral to be. And, if you are
concerned about the effect your eventual death will have on
your family, planning ahead can be a thoughtful and helpful
thing to do.

Sadly, there is another reason that you may be embarking
on planning your own funeral, and that is because you may
have become terminally ill. If this is the case, it will be
immensely difficult for you to have to face the days ahead.
However, taking charge of your funeral may be a way to help
you reclaim an element of control over your life and what is
happening to you.

There are many organisations that are able to offer guidance
and help with sorting out your affairs so do not hesitate to get
in touch with them. Your local church or religious leader will
be delighted to spend time with you talking over what you may
be going through and will endeavour to assist you in finding a
way through. The Natural Death Centre is among those
organisations that also offer support for you and your carers, as
do Age Concern and The Samaritans (see Useful Addresses,
pages 335, 339 and 340 for contact details).

Start with Ideas
First, jot down some general ideas on what you think you
might like; this will help you with everything else that follows.
Think about:
- whether you prefer burial or cremation – or something
  more unusual, such as a burial at sea

- the location of the service or celebration: a church, crematorium chapel or other venue
- whether you want a solid wood, MDF with veneer or eco-friendly (such as cardboard or bamboo) coffin
- whether you would prefer a small, intimate gathering or a larger event
- appropriate music: make a list of your favourite hymns, tunes, songs, psalms, classical music, rock music – even nursery rhymes
- appropriate readings: make a list of your favourite poetry, prose, Bible verses and passages in books
- whether you would like flowers, and which are your favourites, or whether you would prefer guests to donate the money they would have spent to a designated charity
- the general atmosphere you would like to create

Remember that, although this is your funeral, your wishes and ideas are essentially guidance for those who will arrange it. Hopefully, they will always do their best to carry out your wishes but it may not be helpful if these are expressed as fixed directives. Those you leave behind may wish to make their own contribution as an expression of their love. Jot down your ideas in note form as a starting point for when you work on the detail of the plans. If you find any aspects too difficult to contemplate at first, just ignore them and come back to them when you are ready.

Whether or not you have taken out some form of insurance or put aside some cash, work out an approximate budget and stick with it.

Visit local churches and chapels and think about what kind of service you want. If you are not a regular churchgoer or you have no religious inclinations, perhaps you can think of an alternative venue for your funeral.

How Would You Like to be Remembered?

You then might think about how you would like to be remembered.

- look out copies of your favourite photographs of you and your family and friends and perhaps start a 'this-is-your-life' scrapbook
- write down your favourite TV programmes, radio programmes, films, books, DVDs etc.
- write down some occasions that have been particularly important to you and why
- make a list of the people who have been most influential and valuable in your life
- think about whether you would like some kind of a memorial: a gravestone, a plaque, or perhaps a park bench or a tree

You will almost certainly find this a contemplative and moving process. That is to be expected, so don't rush it and don't feel you have to do more than you feel comfortable with at any one time. It may even help you to enjoy your everyday life more because you see how valuable each moment is. It will certainly recall many happy memories and perhaps some poignant ones, too. It may encourage you to get in touch with people you have not seen for some time just because you never got round to calling them. Don't put it off because it may seem, as we have said, a little morbid; it will have plenty of benefits to you in the short term as well as to your family in the long run.

This information will help your family if they want to say a few words about you at the service as it will act as a reminder of what you saw as the most important things in your life.

Newspaper announcements
* an announcement in the local paper is likely to cost from about £30–40
* an announcement in a national paper is likely to start at about £150

They might also like to put an announcement in the local paper, and this will help them know what to say. Full-scale obituaries are usually reserved for 'the great and the good', and of course we wouldn't write our own obituaries anyway. However, if you are a member of a local club, for example, it might like to post an obituary in its magazine or on its website.

The Funeral Service

Despite the fact that not everyone in the UK is a regular churchgoer, in a recent survey, a sizeable percentage of people who were asked said that they would like some kind of church or equivalent religious ceremony before burial or cremation. For many, there is still a sense that the big life events – birth celebration, marriage and death – are closely associated with the church. Closure is important for those left behind and the ritual of ceremony is inextricably linked with that. It is the last thing your partner or your children will be able to do for you, and in the end it is as much for them as it is for you. *You* may not have any particular religious affiliation but it might be cruel to deny your family the feeling that they have been able to say goodbye to you 'properly'.

The Order of Service

If you have ever had to organise a funeral before, you, of all people, will know how difficult this can be. If there is a printer's deadline to be observed, then the order of service has to be arranged very quickly and to the satisfaction of all parties involved. Feelings, which always run high at times like this, can overflow. Family rows that have been threatening for days can break out simply over how many and what hymns and readings have been included. It is often not really an issue over the specific point, but more about the intense emotions that surround such decisions. If you can pre-arrange this for your family, thereby preventing conflict, so much the better.

There is more information on planning a funeral service on pages 96–104 and also on the internet. However, it would be best to discuss the matter with the minister or other person who will lead the service. There are often small variations in the way the clergy and others conduct services.

If you've made a list of favoured hymns and songs, poetry and other readings, you can include the best of those. You might like to leave a few options; you don't have to finalise everything at the beginning.

You might like to put together a draft of the service sheet on your own PC. When it comes to the funeral it can be printed at home or by a professional printer. It is not always necessary to have a printed order of service and not everyone chooses to do so.

Flowers

At most funerals, flowers cover the coffin and are taken to the graveside or displayed just outside the crematorium chapel. The sight of so many beautiful colours and arrangements can serve to uplift the spirit at a very sad time. Wreaths and bouquets are a tangible way in which people can express their love and appreciation and share in the sorrow.

In the gift of flowers, we seem to be connecting with something that resonates deep within us. Flowers are a powerful symbol of human life; they grow and blossom, but also fade and die. Even when it is your wish to have family flowers only, it is not uncommon for other arrangements to turn up. It is wise to be patient and understanding about this. Your preferred wish may be to have the money that would have been spent on flowers donated to a charity. In practice, many people do both.

Burial or Cremation?

Although this is a particularly difficult subject to think about while you are alive and healthy, it can be helpful to your family to know your preference so that they can make the appropriate decision when the time comes.

- Burial is more expensive than cremation, although some people feel happier about the thought of being buried. A grave also provides a focus for the bereaved.
- Cremation is slightly cheaper and dispersal of the ashes can be arranged in a number of traditional and increasingly

original ways. Also, as we are becoming more environmentally aware as a society, the sheer shortage of potential burial space leads an increasing number of us to opt for cremation as a means of disposal. It is quite appropriate to have some kind of a memorial, whether or not it is where your ashes are interred.

Burial

If you decide that you prefer the idea of burial, where would you want to be buried? Identify a place – it might be in the local churchyard, if they can accommodate you. You might prefer the idea of the local municipal cemetery.

Other possibilities for your consideration are the 'green' options – natural burial centres or woodland sites are becoming very popular. You can be buried in one of these lovely places and you or your family can choose a tree or some other form of plant life as your 'headstone'.

You can also be buried on private land providing you have the permission of the landowner and have applied to the Home Office for the right documentation.

There is, or might be, a caveat here. With regard to the natural burial centres, these sites are usually privately owned and in theory it might be possible for a future owner to wish to build a supermarket or other development on the land. The Natural Burial Centre (see Useful Addresses, page 339) says that this will not happen and that deeds of covenant will have been drawn up preventing such an occurrence. If you are considering a woodland burial site, it might be sensible to check with the managers of the site that there is a cast-iron deed of covenant in place to prevent future development.

Cremation

Cremation is an increasingly popular option given that it is usually cheaper than burial and provides more options for the subsequent disposal of the ashes. It can be combined with a church service or a service at the crematorium can be religious in nature.

Alternatively, for people who are ambivalent about the idea of religious input at their funeral, a service at a crematorium can remove God from the equation if that is what is desired. Many crematoria now have chapels without any religious symbols. The users of these places can erect their own religious symbols or just have flowers and pictures and dispense with that side of things altogether. As modern Britain has a multi-cultural identity, it is an advantage to have venues that can accommodate the many rather than the few. Everyone from Christians through to Zen Buddhists can make use of these spaces to say farewell in their own way.

Disposal of cremated remains is easier too. You could have your ashes buried, perhaps in a family grave or some other special place, or you can ask to have them scattered or even dug into your garden. There are also some new and imaginative ways of scattering your ashes. (See Unusual Requests, pages 107–110 and Disposal of Ashes, pages 93–4.)

Choosing a Coffin

You may feel that your family can do this for you in the fullness of time, but with the exorbitant price of some coffins and the pressure that your family may feel to do the best they possibly can by you, it might be sensible to specify roughly what you want. You may indeed want the full works with a luxurious silk-lined solid wood casket, or you might prefer something altogether much simpler. There is a huge range of possibilities from the simplest cardboard coffin, which is not only the cheapest option but is also eminently suitable for those with a concern for the environment, through bamboo coffins, MDF coffins with a variety of wood veneers and then on to the ultimate solid wood casket with brass handles.

Costs of coffins
* a cardboard coffin costs about £70
* a veneered coffin will cost from about £400
* a solid oak coffin will cost from about £700

Reception after the Service and Committal

Most people will want to provide refreshment after the funeral. It is also an opportunity for your family and friends, some of whom may have travelled a long way, to raise a glass to you, share memories and talk to and comfort each other. You can set aside a sum of money for this.

Some people put a 'pot' of money behind the bar in their favourite pub so that the regulars can have a drink on them. Otherwise you could simply leave a little money and give an indication of what you would like, and ask your relatives to organise something appropriate.

Getting Your Wishes Down on Paper

The most important thing of all when planning your own funeral is to get it down on paper – after all, you won't be there to tell anyone yourself!

You can simply write a list and keep it with your will, or you can make a few copies to be distributed to trusted members of the family and friends. If you have started a scrapbook of memorabilia, you could keep your plans all together. If you do this, make sure you put a note with your will about where to find your memories book and tell your close family that you have made it and included your wishes for how your funeral should be organised.

The British are very reluctant to talk about death; it is not part of our modern culture. So you may find that your family appears dismissive when you tell them about your funeral plans: 'You're not going anywhere for years!' or 'Don't be morbid!' are all the type of comments you might expect. Don't be offended. It may be the closest some people get to telling you they love you and don't want to think about losing you. It is also not considered 'polite' to greet such information with an enthusiasm that could be misconstrued. Whether or not they express it, they will certainly be pleased at your care and thoughtfulness, and there is no doubt that it will be a huge help and support to them when the time comes.

PART 2
WHEN A
DEATH OCCURS

WHAT HAPPENS FIRST

When someone dies, there are many practical things that need to be done in a relatively short time. It is not easy when you are having to cope with the emotional trauma of losing a loved one, so what follows is designed to help you through the practical issues with as few problems as possible.

This section looks at what happens in the first few hours so you have some idea what to expect and what is expected of you.

Death at Home

Many of us hope that we will, in the fullness of time, be able to die peacefully at home. If a person does die at home, then the procedures are usually relatively straightforward.

It may sound strange but it is not always obvious that someone has died. Death can be very quiet and peaceful so, if you suspect that your loved one has passed away, you should call a doctor for confirmation. The doctor will perform the necessary checks to verify death and, providing the doctor saw the deceased in the fortnight prior to the death, he or she will be able to issue a Medical Certificate of Cause of Death straight away. If the death was sudden or unexpected, then further investigation may be necessary – but don't worry about this, it is just to ascertain beyond doubt the cause of death.

If someone has died at home, you may find that something called rigor mortis has set in. We are all familiar with this term, and will probably have a vague idea of its meaning, but it is also likely that we will have little understanding of the real process. Rigor mortis (a Latin term meaning the stiffness of death) is a gradual stiffening of the muscles that begins about six hours after death and works its way through the entire body in 24 hours. After this period, the rigor mortis wears off and the body relaxes again. This is why it can be used as an indicator of the time of death.

A condition called hypostasis also occurs. If you have the deceased at home, do not be alarmed by what appears to be heavy bruising forming on the body. This is merely the blood in the body settling to all the lowest points due to the forces of gravity.

You should call a funeral director straight away. They will tell you exactly what to do and come to the house to take charge of the arrangements that need to be taken care of. They are most likely to remove the body to their premises where they can care for the body.

Death in Hospital or a Hospice

If death takes place when a patient is in hospital, and if you aren't there at the time, then the nursing staff will ensure that you or the next of kin and members of the immediate family are informed as soon as possible. If you were present at the moment of death, then you will have realised that death is often very peaceful, even easy, particularly if the person who has died was very ill and possibly under sedation.

If the death was from natural causes, the body will then be taken to the hospital mortuary after a doctor has established the details (time, date and cause) of the death. A Medical Certificate of Cause of Death will be issued by the hospital authorities. This will usually be signed by the doctor who was in attendance prior to the patient's death.

In some cases, the hospital may wish to carry out a post-mortem examination to ascertain the exact cause of death, but only if the next of kin agrees. This procedure does not involve the coroner.

Organ Donation

It is also at this point that relatives of the deceased may be asked about organ donation. Any patient who has died in hospital, provided he or she was under the age of 75 and had been in good health until the moment of death, will be considered a suitable donor for organ transplant.

The nature of the procedure means that it must be performed very quickly after death has occurred. This can be difficult for relatives to contemplate so soon after their loss but if you appreciate why the doctors need to press for a quick decision, it does make it easier to understand.

Hearts, lungs, kidneys, livers and corneas are always in demand and there is a huge shortage of suitable organs, so if you know that your loved one carried a donor card or that he or she would be happy to help someone else in this way, it makes your decision to give approval that much easier. People often say that there is also comfort to be drawn from someone else being able to live on as a result of this most generous gift.

However, if you feel that you are unable to give permission, then you are quite within your rights to refuse. You must make the decision that you feel is right at the time and then move on, not dwell on whether you should have made a different choice.

Another, possibly more difficult, decision in this context may be if the patient is pronounced brain dead but is being kept 'alive' on a life-support system. If under the age of 75, he or she will also be considered a suitable donor for organ transplant. In this case, you will have more time to think about the options and discuss them with the doctors before you make your final decision. It is an important decision that requires careful thought and time.

Post Mortems

These occur only if there is some doubt about the cause of death, for example if it was sudden or unexpected. You will have to sign a consent form, which used to state that 'tissues may be retained for diagnostic, teaching and research purposes'. In 1999 it came to light that a number of hospitals had retained the organs from children without the knowledge or consent of the parents. After exhaustive investigation into the practice, procedures have now been altered. If a post mortem is necessary, you can rest assured that the strict guidelines that now govern these procedures will be scrupulously observed.

Donating the Body for Medical Research
If it was the intention of the deceased to donate their body for the advancement of medical science, then they should have applied for and filled in the appropriate forms. If this was not done but you know that your loved one wanted their body to be used in this way, then you will have to fill in the forms yourself. Inform the hospital authorities at once as you will need to contact HM Inspector of Anatomy (see Useful Addresses, page 338) as soon as possible after death has taken place, though the hospital may be able to do this for you.

Unfortunately, not all bodies will be accepted for medical research, so it might be wise for you and your family to make some preliminary funeral arrangements for the deceased just in case. If the body is accepted, then the medical school in question will arrange for it to be collected. The death should then be registered in the normal way (see Registering the Death, pages 67–75).

Since there will be no need for a funeral, you may wish to organise a service of thanksgiving.

Laying Out the Body or the Last Offices
Laying out the body, or the last offices, are rather archaic-sounding terms that refer to the washing and tidying of the body that takes place after death. When someone dies in hospital, then the staff there will wash the body: if the death took place at home, then the funeral director will do this.

The funeral director will also be responsible for the remaining tasks: the eyes and mouth will need to be closed, and the bodily orifices stopped with cotton wool. (The funeral director will call the washing and preparation of the body, the 'first offices' as it is the first task they perform.)

If you wish, the funeral director can arrange for the laying-out team to wash and set a woman's hair, apply make-up to her face and dress her in her favourite clothes. Men will need to be shaved as hair continues to grow for some time after death. With regard to dress, if you would prefer not to have the deceased dressed in his or her own clothes, then the funeral director will provide a simple shroud for a fee.

DEATH IN UNUSUAL CIRCUMSTANCES

Most people will not need to consult the information in this chapter but those who have experienced a loss in unusual circumstances will find this useful when coping with the specific issues involved.

When Death Occurs Abroad

If the death has occurred overseas, either as a result of illness or an accident, you should contact the local police at once, as well as the nearest British Embassy or Consulate. If you are staying in a hotel or you are part of a package holiday, inform the hotel manager as well as your holiday representative and ask for a doctor to attend.

If you are in a country where English is not widely spoken and you are not fluent in the local language, difficulties and misunderstandings might arise; to avoid these and further distress, ask for an interpreter as well.

Although it will be very difficult for you, try to remain calm. You will need the deceased's passport, travel documents and insurance policy. Keep these with you at all times from now on, along with your own, and every time you are asked for them, make sure they are all returned to you. If they do have to be taken away from you for any reason, ask for a receipt and the name of the person who has taken them.

If you and the deceased are insured, full details of what to do in any event, including death, should be found on the policy itself. If in any doubt, call the helpline number, which should also be listed on the document. The insurance company should be able to wire you an advance straight away for any immediate expenses. Unfortunately, the British Consulate will not be able to cover any costs, nor will it be able to pay for any doctors, ambulances or other incidental costs incurred by the death. It will, however, arrange a loan, provided you are able to prove you have the funds available at home and are able to repay. You will probably have to sign some kind of letter or form acknowledging your liability in the matter, and that all monies loaned will be repaid by you.

You may have to register the death in the country where it took place, and you should then be issued with the appropriate documentation. After this, the death must be recorded at the Embassy or Consulate, where it will be entered in the Register of Foreign Deaths. It is essential you do this, particularly if you are planning to bring the body home, as otherwise there will be no record in the UK of the death, and you may encounter difficulties when trying to organise a burial or cremation. There is another vital reason for you to do this as, unless you have recorded the death at the Embassy or Consulate, you will be unable to make any claim on your insurance.

Transportation of the Body
Bringing the body home will prove very expensive and may not be covered by your insurance policy, so do check it carefully. If you find you are not covered for this eventuality and that you do not have enough money in accounts at home either, you have two options open to you:

- you can bury the deceased locally
- you can opt for cremation locally, and then bring the ashes home yourself, although you should note that cremation is not available in all countries

If you do decide to bring the body home, you have a few choices: you can call a reputable funeral director, such as Co-operative Funeralcare (see Useful Addresses, page 336), for advice, and they can help make the arrangements for you. Whatever happens, you will need permission from the local authorities to remove the body from their jurisdiction and certain procedures must be implemented before removal can take place. A body must be embalmed and a certificate of embalming provided. The body must be placed in a metal-lined coffin, which must then be packaged in the appropriate way – the airline and local authorities will be able to advise you on this. You will also need all the necessary paperwork to be in order for customs clearance at both ends of the journey. These papers must remain with the body at all stages of the journey. You will also need to make arrangements with the airline to ensure that it is prepared to repatriate the body for you. Once back on UK soil, and with customs dealt with, the body should be removed from the airport as soon as possible to a funeral directors.

When Death Occurs in the Air

When death occurs in an aircraft it is considered to have taken place in the country to which the plane belongs.

The matter will be dealt with swiftly when the plane lands. The captain of the aircraft will have radioed ahead to ensure that the authorities on the ground are forewarned and you will be met and advised of your options on arrival.

If the death takes place on the outward journey, you will be met at your destination by the British Consul; if you are inbound, then the local police and an official from the coroner's office will meet you and discuss with you what will happen next.

When Death Occurs at Sea

If death takes place on a foreign ship, then it will count as a death abroad.

The death will be recorded in the ship's log, and the ship's captain must advise the harbour authorities before arrival in the next port. The nearest British Consul should be informed as soon as the ship docks.

If the ship is British, the death will be recorded in the ship's log and the information will be passed to the Registry of

Shipping and Seamen at the next port. The Master (or Captain) will decide what to do with the body. It may happen – perhaps for health reasons or due to lack of mortuary facilities, for example – that the Master has to order a burial at sea. In most cases however, if the death is sudden and unexplained, he will try to keep the body in cold storage in case of a coroner's enquiry.

Copies of the Death Certificate may be obtained from the Registry of Shipping and Seamen.

Death as a Result of Terrorist Attack

Although this sort of death is thankfully rare, since the events of 7 July 2005 in London and 9/11 in the United States it is now an issue that sadly requires consideration.

Death as a result of terrorist attack will be dealt with according to the laws of the country in which it took place. In remoter areas, where the infrastructure is different from that in Britain, the formalities may take longer than usual; each country, however, will have its own way of coping with such a situation and one can only be patient and wait for the eventual outcome.

Helplines and other enquiry services are set up by the Foreign Office as soon as is practicably possible in the event of a terrorist outrage, and all news will be passed on as soon as it is available.

The Foreign Office will assist with the repatriation of the body and will advise you on what to do after that, along with details of costs, if there are any.

Violent Death

Fortunately, very few people have to confront this dreadful circumstance and those who do will be offered a great deal of professional help and support. These few notes should give you some guidance on what to expect but are in no way comprehensive.

- In any violent death, the police will almost certainly be involved.

- If you should come across the dead body of a stranger or even of someone you know, and you feel instinctively that things are not right, inform the police straight away.
- If the person is obviously dead, do not touch the body or anything near the body, and do not allow anyone else to touch the body or anything near the body and its environs until the police have made a full inspection of the scene. If the death is suspicious, the police will need to secure the area and will also need a full statement from you.
- If you come across a person who looks as if they might have been electrocuted, whatever you do, do not approach or touch the body. Call the emergency services at once and then try to turn off the power supply.
- The coroner is also likely to be involved in a case of violent death and there will almost certainly be an inquest, and possibly an eventual trial.
- Ask for advice and support from the police. They will have previous experience of dealing with such situations and will have trained staff and systems in place to help you.
- Whatever your involvement, be prepared for media intrusion and public curiosity. Unfortunately neither will respect your grief – both will want to witness it. Be firm and consistent in keeping the press at bay.

Stillbirth

A stillborn child is one born after 24 weeks of pregnancy and, although it is very painful and difficult, at present in England and Wales both the birth and the death must be registered within 42 days. The registrations of both can be done in a single procedure at the Registrar for Births, Marriages and Deaths.

The doctor or a certified midwife who was in attendance at the birth can issue a Certificate of Stillbirth. If neither a doctor nor a midwife was present, then one of the parents or another qualified informant can make the declaration on Form 35, available at the Registrar of Births, Marriages and Deaths.

If there are any doubts about the birth – perhaps the child was born alive but died soon after birth – then the coroner must be informed. This is traumatic for the parents but essential to establish what went wrong.

The Coroner

Occasionally a death may have to be reported to the coroner. The coroner is responsible for investigating certain deaths and must follow certain guidelines. He or she:

- will arrange for a post-mortem examination of the body; the consent of the next of kin is not required for this, though the relatives of the deceased can elect a doctor to be present
- will not take any action if the cause of death falls outside his or her guidelines
- will order an inquest or a Fatal Accident Inquiry (FAI) if the death:
  o was violent
  o was by suicide
  o was sudden or unexplained and the post-mortem results remain uncertain
  o took place while the deceased was in police custody or prison
  o took place on an operating table or whilst under anaesthesia
  o took place during a termination of pregnancy
  o was caused by drug abuse or poison
  o was caused directly or indirectly by an accident

There should be no costs to the family of the deceased if a coroner's investigation is necessary.

Although the coroner does not need to seek permission from the family of the deceased for a post mortem, if the family objects, for example, on religious grounds, it may make representations to him or her. The coroner may still feel it necessary to proceed with a post mortem, but will continue only if in the belief that it is in the public interest as well as in the interests of the deceased and his or her family. This will inevitably be distressing for the family members but the coroner will proceed with sensitivity to their feelings.

Post Mortem Examination or Autopsy

Post mortem is a Latin term meaning 'after death'; autopsy comes from the Greek autoptes, which means 'eye-witness'. The purpose of an autopsy or post-mortem examination, should one be required, is to establish the true cause of death if there are any question marks. However, the fact that an autopsy is requested does not necessarily mean that there are any suspicious circumstances, and the authorities may tend to err on the side of caution. Before any post-mortem examination takes place, the family will be informed and all the relevant information and procedures will be explained as carefully and tactfully as possible.

Inquests

An inquest will be called in the event of a death taking place unexpectedly. The circumstances surrounding an unexpected death, sometimes called 'sudden death', vary, and an inquest or enquiry has to be held in each case to establish the medical cause and the circumstances surrounding such a death. The coroner is in charge of an inquest and it is his or her duty to hold the enquiry in such a way as to best serve the interests of the public, the relatives and the deceased.

The Coroner's Court is not involved in any business other than establishing the cause of death, so if an inquest is deemed necessary after the death of a member of your family, please do not worry.

Relatives are allowed to attend and may ask questions of witnesses with the coroner's permission. The relatives can also be represented by a lawyer. It may be wise to have a lawyer present, particularly if the death was caused by a road accident or an industrial incident, either of which might lead to a claim for compensation. You are not, however, entitled to legal aid for this kind of assistance.

The usual form for an enquiry begins with the coroner opening a short inquest to record the death and to identify the deceased. The inquest is then adjourned. If disposal of the body will not prejudice his or her enquiries, the coroner will issue the appropriate certificate required for burial or cremation. The family is then able to get on with the business of organising the funeral. The coroner will resume the inquest at a later date.

An open verdict will be called where there is no conclusive evidence available (for example, suspected suicide).

An organisation called Inquest exists to help families involved with coroners and their enquiries; it has a helpline and also publishes helpful information (see Useful Addresses, page 338).

REGISTERING THE DEATH

After the doctor has issued you with the Medical Certificate of Cause of Death, you or the next of kin must register the death with the Registrar of Births, Marriages and Deaths.

This must be done as soon as possible and is a legal requirement. You will not be able to bury or cremate the deceased until you have done this. In England, Wales and Northern Ireland, you should have registered the death within five days. In Scotland you must register within eight days. In some cases you will be given a further nine days, providing the registrar has received, in writing, confirmation that a Medical Certificate of Cause of Death has been signed by the doctor.

When the attending doctor has issued you with a Medical Certificate of Cause of Death, you can go to the Registrar of Births, Marriages and Deaths. Look in the phone book to locate your nearest registry; alternatively, your doctor's surgery will be able to tell you where the registry is and its hours of opening.

Take the certificate the doctor has given you and make sure you have enough money to pay the required fees. Most registration districts operate a first-come first-served system, but increasingly there are some, in busier areas, where an appointments system is now in place. However, you should be able to wait and the registrar will see you when he or she is next free.

The doctor's certificate comes in two parts: one is submitted to the registrar, the other is handed back to you. If the registrar thinks the information on the certificate is insufficient, he or she may refer the death to the coroner, or to the procurator fiscal if the death occurred in Scotland. The registrar may also refer the death to the coroner if the doctor who signed the death certificate did not see the deceased in the 14 days before death. It might be upsetting if this has to happen, but there is nothing to worry about; it is only to ensure that there has been no foul play and that the cause of death is established beyond all doubt.

You will also be required to provide:

- the full names of the deceased, and any other names he or she has been known by, including a woman's maiden name
- his or her date and place of birth
- his or her most recent occupation and, if the person who has died was a married woman, her husband's name and occupation

You will also have to confirm the place and date of death. In Scotland, the time of death will be required as well. Other questions will be asked, such as the date of birth of any surviving spouse and information regarding state pensions and allowances the person might have been receiving, including war pensions. You should also provide the person's NHS number and medical card if possible; however, if you have been unable to locate either the number or the card, do not worry.

The death will then be entered in a register of deaths and you can have a certified copy of the entry – the Death Certificate. There is a fee for this certificate.

You will be given a Certificate for Burial or Cremation, sometimes called the Green Form. This must be handed over to the funeral director in due course, as generally speaking the funeral cannot proceed without this first having happened. If the deceased is to be cremated, then the crematorium authority will need to see it in order for the cremation to go ahead.

If the coroner is dealing with you, having completed the enquiries, he or she will give you an Order for Burial (or Form 101) or a Certificate for Cremation (or Form E). These give permission to the relevant authority for burial or cremation to take place. It should be taken to the funeral director.

You will also be given a Death Certificate for sending to the Department of Social Security (DSS). Details of the death appear on one side and on the reverse is a claims form, should you be in need of assistance with funeral expenses and so on.

Note: As you will need several copies of the Death Certificate for a number of purposes – with regard to the will, informing banks and building societies, any claims for life insurance etc. – it is worth asking for them now. It is less expensive to get copies now than if you apply for more later.

Copies of the Death Certificate
* the current charge for each copy of a Death Certificate is £3.50 if ordered at the time of issue
* the cost will be £7 per copy if ordered later

If you are unable to attend the registry office in the district in which the person died, you can register the death elsewhere. The details will then be passed on to the registrar in the right district for issuing the certificates.

Who Can Register a Death?

If you are sharing the responsibility for dealing with these practical issues, which is always helpful at this difficult time, a number of people are able to register the death:

- a relative of the deceased who was present at the death
- a relative of the deceased who saw him or her during the last illness
- a relative of the deceased who is living or staying in the district where the death occurred
- a person present at the death
- the occupier (meaning a hospital doctor, care home matron, prison governor etc.), if he or she has knowledge of the death
- any resident/inmate of an institution such as a care home or prison, if he or she has knowledge of the death

- the person causing the disposal of the body (i.e. the person responsible for the funeral)

A death that didn't occur at home or in hospital or any other institution can be registered by:

- a relative of the deceased who has knowledge of the particulars required to register a death
- a person who was present at the death
- a person who found the body, if the death was sudden or suspicious
- the person who is responsible for the funeral

Registration in Scotland

The rules governing the procedures following a death are essentially the same as they are in England. There are a few variations, but these are mostly linguistic differences. The person known as the coroner in England, for example, is known in Scotland as the procurator fiscal.

Registering a Death

In Scotland, the death must be registered within eight days – slightly longer than the allowed period in England. The person who reports the death must be either:

- a relative of the deceased
- a person present at the death
- the executor of the deceased (or any other legal representative)
- the person in charge of the premises where death took place
- any person who knows the details pertaining to the death

The death may be registered in either:

- the district where the death took place
- the district where the deceased usually stayed

If a person died while visiting Scotland, then the death must be registered where the death took place.

The procedure for registering a death is, as it is in England and Wales, a Q&A routine, except in Scotland the registrar will require slightly more information. As well as the Medical

Certificate of Cause of Death, the person reporting the death must also provide:

- the date, place and time of death
- confirmation of whether the deceased had ever been married
- the name, surname and occupation of each spouse if there was more than one
- the name and occupation of the deceased's father and the name, maiden name and occupation of the deceased's mother, if those parents are still alive

Registering a Stillbirth

A stillbirth that occurred in Scotland must be registered within 21 days. If no doctor or midwife can issue the appropriate certificate, then the person reporting the event must fill in a special document, Form 7. A stillbirth can be registered in the district in which the stillbirth took place or in the district in which the mother normally resided.

A stillbirth must have been registered before any burial or cremation can take place.

The registrar will need:

- a doctor's or a midwife's certificate or Form 7
- the date, time and place of the stillbirth
- where applicable, the place and date of the parents' marriage

All stillbirths and neonatal deaths are reported to the procurator fiscal, who will in due course report the results of his or her findings to the Registrar General.

Certificate of Registration

The informant (the person who is responsible for registering the death) will be given a Certificate of Registration of Death, also known as Form 14. This should be given to the funeral director to give either to the crematorium authority or to the cemetery authority. There is no fee payable for this certificate.

The registrar also issues a registration or Notification of Death form, which can be used for National Insurance and DSS requirements. This certificate is free, but all others will have to be paid for.

As in England and Wales, it would be wise to order copies of death certificates at the time of registration, as they will be cheaper than if you order them later.

New Certification Procedures

Following a number of recent scandals, most particularly the Harold Shipman affair, the Home Office has been reviewing the procedures for the certification of death. It is necessary to reassure the public that those in authority are completely answerable and, in view of this, along with reviews of the coroner system, it is hoped that more stringent legislation will soon be in place.

There will be other additions to existing rules, namely:

- The inclusion of a person who will be named as 'life-partner' amongst those already eligible to register a death.
- The same information for men and for women is now to be included, i.e. marital status plus name and occupation of spouse.
- New provision for the registration of certain deaths at sea.
- The use of the Welsh language is to be extended.
- Registration of stillbirth can be made within one year and there will be an extension of persons eligible to register the stillbirth.

The legislative changes are expected to be in place during 2005 and the new system will be phased in as soon as is practicable.

Who Else Needs to Know?

If you are the person who is responsible for organising the funeral, one of the duties that may fall to you is that of informing family, friends, colleagues and acquaintances of the sad news. However, until you have a firm date for the funeral, initially you will need to inform only family and close friends. It is a difficult task, as you will find yourself having to tell the story over and over again and, while some may find this therapeutic, others could find it distressing. If you fall into the latter category, do detail some other family members to help you with this particular job. If you do find telephoning people upsetting, you can always write or send letters or e-mails. This may seem impersonal, but most people will not be offended, particularly under the circumstances.

It might also help if you were able to locate the address book belonging to the deceased as you will then be able to ensure you don't miss anyone out.

Once you have set a date for the funeral then all the other remoter friends and acquaintances can be informed and invited to the funeral at the same time.

Informing Financial and Legal Institutions

The people and institutions that need to know immediately about the death are as follows:

- doctor (if he or she has not already been informed)
- employer
- bank and building society manager(s) – have to hand details of account numbers
- credit card and/or store-card companies – have to hand account numbers
- solicitor
- pension holders
- insurance companies
- Department of Social Security
- stockbrokers

- possible creditors
- mortgage companies
- landlord (if the deceased was living in rented accommodation)
- utilities providers
- local authority (with regard to council tax)

Securing the Property of the Deceased

If your sole remaining parent or another single close relative has died and you do not or did not live at the same address, it is vital that you take immediate action to ensure the property is secure now that it is empty. If there is any doubt as to who should take responsibility for doing this, then you need to communicate with relatives, friends or neighbours to ensure there is no confusion. Word will get round quickly, particularly in a small community, that your father or your mother or your aunt has passed away – and that where they lived now stands empty. Unfortunately your sad loss will be no deterrent to the criminal fraternity, who will only see the possibility of an undisturbed break-in.

You can always stay in the property yourself, while the affairs of the deceased are sorted out, or you could try asking someone to house-sit. If neither of these is possible, then hopefully kind neighbours will be prepared to keep an eye on things for you. You can, in the meantime, take all the necessary precautions against potential burglary.

- Inform the police that the house is empty and give them your name, address and phone number as the key-holder.
- Make sure all doors and windows have adequate and working locks and use them.
- Any security or burglar alarm should be activated; inform any other keyholders if you do this.
- Install a few time-activated lights as a deterrent.
- Make sure any cars are locked and garaged if possible or, if not, immobilised. You can do this by the removal of a small

car part. If you are unsure how to do this, your local garage will be able to advise you.

- Lock any garden gates or other means of access.
- Switch off and unplug all electrical appliances in the house, except the fridge and possibly the freezer if there is one. You may decide to have a reception at the house after the funeral and will need it then. You will also need it, along with the kettle, to store basic supplies (milk, butter etc.) during the house-clearing at a later date.
- For the time being, leave the heating on low – slightly higher in winter. It may be expensive to keep it on in an empty house, but it will prevent damp and degradation to the property, which will be important if you are to sell the house. It will also prevent burst pipes during a cold snap, and that will be much more expensive than any heating bill.
- Cancel deliveries of milk, papers etc.
- Inform the Royal Mail as soon as possible. There will be a small charge for this.
- Dead house-plants on a windowsill are a give-away, so if you can't get in regularly to water them, remove them.
- Finally, dispose of all perishable goods such as fruit, vegetables and bread which will go off quickly and make the house smell. If the deceased had been ill and there are cut flowers in vases from well-wishers, throw those away too and rinse out the vases with warm soapy water.

The idea should be to make the house look as normal and as inhabited as possible.

Pets

Any pets will need to be re-homed. Do treat animals with sympathy and kindness as they are creatures of habit and their world will have been turned inexplicably upside-down. If you cannot take them in yourself or are unable to find a good home locally, please contact your local RSPCA or PDSA. You will find their numbers in the Yellow Pages and they will be able to advise you.

ARRANGING A FUNERAL

Once the formalities are over, and you have registered the death and informed all the relevant authorities of the circumstances, you can begin to put together the funeral.

Even if you have no religious inclination, there should nevertheless be some sort of ceremony, not only for you, but also for others. The rituals surrounding death have always been important to mankind, and there is some evidence that these offices contribute enormously to the recovery process after bereavement. In short, it is important to say goodbye properly. A brief and perfunctory funeral may ultimately leave you feeling that you didn't do enough and may only increase any feelings of guilt, which can anyway be common after you lose someone.

The Office of Fair Trading has launched online advice for those who are arranging a funeral and it is worth consulting the site to make sure you are getting a fair deal (see Useful Addresses, page 339). Useful information and news is also available at www.uk-funerals.co.uk.

If you are in the position where you are organising a funeral for the first time, you may be feeling rather overwhelmed by the size of the task in front of you. There is so much to do and in such a short time. You will also be coping with your own feelings of shock and grief. This chapter is designed to help you navigate your way through the procedures.

There are three things to consider before you begin to make plans for a funeral:

- costs
- timing
- whether to appoint a funeral director or arrange the funeral yourself

Costs

We all want to give our loved ones the best possible send-off when they die. It's the last thing you will do for them and this ritual is as important as any in life.

It may therefore seem distasteful to refer to money at this early stage, but the simple truth is that most of us are on a budget and, unless money is no object or you have special funds set aside for this purpose, it must be at the top of the list of considerations. Unfortunately, everything to do with funerals has a price tag attached so you do need to be practical; if your budget is slim then choosing a sumptuous casket might mean that you could bankrupt the estate of the deceased. Every funeral director will have a range of funeral packages to suit most budgets, but do not be afraid to shop around so that you can get a sense of what's on offer in the marketplace.

Average funeral costs

Over the last 10 years, the costs for burial have risen by about 140 per cent, compared with a rise of 67 per cent for cremations. Costs vary hugely across the country, with London and the Home Counties being the most expensive.

* funeral with burial £2,500–3,000
* funeral with cremation £1,700–2,000

There are various ways to fund a funeral:

- from the deceased's pre-paid funeral plan
- from the deceased's bank or building society funds
- from an insurance policy of the deceased that might cover the expense of the funeral
- state entitlements
- charity funds
- a loan

It may be that the deceased has left behind a pre-paid funeral plan or some other form of insurance, so do hunt around to see if you can find anything like this.

If the deceased was the main breadwinner then his or her accounts will have been frozen, although the bank manager will probably allow the withdrawal of funds to cover the costs of the funeral providing there is enough in the account. You will have to produce an original copy of the Death Certificate, but you will have to show this anyway when you contact the bank regarding the change in circumstances. If you and the deceased had a joint bank account, you should be able to draw on that account without any difficulty.

Check the deceased's financial details to see if he or she had a life or other insurance policy that might provide funds for the funeral. All companies will have a help or information line so you can ask what the policy covers.

You may be eligible for State benefits or some other State assistance with the costs (see below).

If you do not have the funds and are not eligible for help, you may have to consider taking out a loan. Your bank or your building society may well be sympathetic and, if the value of the deceased's estate can bear it, you may be able to reclaim the costs later.

Government Support
It is your right to claim State benefits if you are eligible, so you should not feel embarrassed to do so. Your local benefits office will give you guidance and advice and there are leaflets explaining your entitlement. Staff at the Department of Social Security (DSS) are always kind and sympathetic and will do their best to help. The DSS can also refer you to charities where you may be able to get the help you need if for some reason you don't qualify for state assistance. In addition, your funeral director should initially establish with you how you intend to pay and if there is a problem he or she will be able to advise you further.

As the person responsible for arranging the funeral you may be eligible for help from government funds. The DSS produces leaflets, which include information about Social Fund payments:

- D49 What to do after Death in England and Wales
- D49s What to do after Death in Scotland
- SB16 A Guide to the Social Fund

> **Social Fund payments**
> * for eligible applicants, payments of up to £2,000 can be
>   made from the Social Fund towards the funeral costs

You may be entitled to help if you have arranged the
funeral in the UK and the deceased had his or her main home
in the UK at the time of death. You may, occasionally, be
entitled to help if you have arranged the funeral elsewhere in
the European Union.

Whether or not help will be available depends largely on
your financial status. Unfortunately, even if the deceased was
on benefits, that will have no bearing on any decision. Awards
will not be considered if there is a close relative who can afford
to pay for the funeral. The relevant Benefits Agency form
(SF200) can be obtained at your local benefits office or online.
For further information and recent updates you can contact
your local DSS office or visit the Department for Work and
Pensions' website at www.dwp.gov.uk.

You can get help if you (or your partner) receive any of the
following benefits:
- Income Support
- Income-based Job-Seeker's Allowance
- Housing Benefit
- Council Tax Benefit
- Working Families' Tax Credit
- Disabled Person's Tax Credit

The DSS doesn't usually commit itself to contributing
towards your costs until the funeral director has issued the
funeral account *after* the funeral has taken place. If the DSS
decides to turn down your application, you will then be
responsible for the outstanding amount due to the funeral

director. Obviously this is very unsatisfactory but that is how matters stand at the moment. All DSS information is also subject to change so do please check with your local Benefits Agency, where staff will be pleased to offer the latest information and advice on what to do next.

There is a low-price funeral package available at most funeral directors, designed to provide a complete funeral for the full amount the DSS is prepared to pay. The funeral payment in this case will cover:

- the cost of re-opening an existing grave or of opening a new grave; OR the cost of cremation
- the cost of necessary certificates
- the cost of removing pacemakers and/or other medical devices prior to cremation
- the cost of documents needed for the release of the assets of the deceased
- the cost of the transportation of the body (within the UK) when it is over a distance of 80 km/50 miles
- the cost of the return journey for you to arrange the funeral and then attend the same
- an allowance for any other funeral expenses

Additional expenses
* a low-cost funeral package will allow up to £700 for any other expenses in connection with the funeral

---

If there is a funeral plan that the deceased began but didn't complete, the DSS may be able to help you, so take the original plan documents to your local office plus anything else that may assist them in making a decision.

A payment from the Social Fund will eventually have to be paid back from the estate of the deceased, provided such funds are available. The DSS does not count the value of the home occupied by the partner of the deceased or personal mementoes left to friends and relatives.

Timing

Funerals usually take place within a week after death, though this is not an absolute rule that has to be observed. If a death has taken place during a public holiday for example, then the funeral may not take place for as much as 10 days afterwards. If the family wishes for any reason to delay the funeral, then it need not take place for a considerable length of time, though there would be cost implications relating to additional services the funeral director would have to provide.

You will therefore have a little time in which to gather your thoughts, consult family and friends and decide on what you would like, as well as what you think the deceased might have wanted, and whether to appoint a funeral director or make the funeral a much more personal affair by arranging everything yourself.

You can spend too long focusing on one particular issue that may be troubling you, such as whether or not you have chosen the right coffin, so one solution might be to make yourself a timetable to ensure that everything is addressed. Don't give yourself so much to do that you end up feeling exhausted. Delegate tasks to family and friends, who will probably be only too pleased to help.

Funeral Director Arranged or Self-organised

The easiest and by far the most usual option is to put yourself in the capable hands of a funeral director. However, you may wish to take on the task of arranging the funeral yourself as a last tribute to someone you love. Both these options are covered in full below.

Funeral Director

Most funeral directors have a range of packages that suit most budgets and, to find out what is available, it may be worth your while spending a little time either telephoning or calling on the companies in your area. You will then be able to choose the funeral that suits you best as well as the firm you like best. It is important to feel that you will get on with the people involved and that they will handle everything in the most sensitive and sympathetic way. One would hope that all funeral directors will be kind and will treat you with the utmost tact and sympathy. They are used to dealing with the bereaved, after all.

Once you have made your choice, you should let the selected firm know at once so that they can come to collect the body if the deceased died at home, or go to collect it from the hospital or nursing home if they died there. Most funeral directors will try to ensure that the person with whom you have first point of contact will take charge of the funeral from then on and he or she will remain in charge until after the funeral has taken place.

The funeral director collects the body in a specially adapted vehicle. If the deceased has passed away at home, all funeral directors will make every effort to remove the body with care and discretion. They will either place the body on a stretcher with a cover, or in a lightweight coffin specially designed for the purpose. The body will then be taken to the funeral director's mortuary, where it will be laid out before being taken to the firm's own chapel of rest. This is a small room on the premises where the body is laid in a coffin until just before the funeral. Family and friends may come and see the body at any time during this period. Family members who weren't able to say goodbye may like to take this opportunity to do so now. If you or any member of the family and any friends wish to see the body before the funeral, please let the funeral director know so that they can ensure that you are given the proper attention and that any questions you may have can be answered. Sometimes families may wish to place a few items in the coffin, such as small mementoes, photographs or flowers. Some funeral directors may make a small charge for viewing in the evenings and/or at weekends.

After the body has been taken away, the funeral director will contact you and will either call on you at home or invite you to the funeral home to discuss the funeral and any requirements you have. He or she should at this point discuss finances with you and how you intend to pay but will do so discreetly and with tact. While it may, on the face of things, seem rather insensitive, it is important to establish straight away what the parameters are. It will also help him or her to guide you towards the most suitable choices for your budget. The usual basic funeral will include the following:

- the services of the funeral director
- all arrangements
- provision of the necessary staff to attend the funeral
- provision of a suitable coffin
- transport of the body from the place to death to the funeral home
- care of the body
- transport of the body to where the funeral service is taking place and, if necessary, to the cemetery or crematorium afterwards
- burial or cremation arrangements

The basic funeral fee will not include embalming, viewing the deceased (where a fee is payable), provision of limousines or other cars, or any other additional fees that may be incurred.

When making these financial enquiries, if you think the estate of the deceased will not be able to bear the cost of the funeral, and if you are unable to meet those costs yourself, the funeral director will ask you to see if there might be a pre-paid funeral plan, or if there might be any other relatives who would be willing to pay for it. You may qualify for a payment from the Social Fund and your funeral director will be able to advise you on how to go about applying for help.

Once you have both agreed on how to proceed, the funeral director will normally pay all expenses, including additional fees to doctors, clergy and crematoria or cemetery authorities, and in some cases will deal with all the additional expenses such as placing announcements in the papers, printing of service sheets and catering. These will all be included in the final bill but he or she should give you a written estimate before you finally agree to go ahead. You will then usually need to pay a deposit.

The funeral director will have a catalogue of coffins from which you can choose the most appropriate for your loved one, as well as a limited selection of fresh floral tributes that the firm can also arrange for you. All funeral directors will, or should, have clear price lists regardless of whether costs are a factor or not. If you cannot see one, please ask for a price list before making any final decisions.

Making Your Own Arrangements

When a death occurs, most people use the services of a funeral director. They are the experts who are trained to deal with all the issues around death, funerals and burial, including the preparation and handling of a dead body. They also know most of the legal requirements and administrative procedures.

It has not always been the case that funeral directors were available. In past centuries, the family took care of all the funeral arrangements on their own or with the help of friends, from making the coffin and 'laying out' the body to digging the grave.

There are today some families or individuals who value the opportunity to take a more active and direct role in the funeral arrangements from the moment of death. A 'do-it-yourself' approach can feel more personal and special but it is not a decision that should be entered into lightly. Apart from the emotional and psychological pressures of making all the arrangements yourself, caring for a dead body and preparation for burial is quite a skilled task. There are also rules and regulations about where and how people can be buried. It would be essential to check what is both possible and legal.

Understandably, some people feel they would like to have a more personal involvement in the disposing of their loved ones. It is, after all, one of the last expressions of love you can show. There are a great many ways in which you can take an active role in managing the arrangements. The important thing is to do what feels right and comfortable for you within the rules and regulations. Whether this is handling most of the tasks yourself or getting a funeral director to make most of the arrangements is a matter of choice.

The Organic Funeral

Many people are now very aware of the impact of our modern lifestyle on the planet and there are those who are deeply committed to making a difference. Having an organic funeral – one that tries to adhere to environmentally friendly principles – is a relatively recent development but it is becoming very popular. Thanks to high-profile campaigners such as the Prince of Wales, an organic way of life is now acceptable, and there is nothing remotely odd about wanting to ensure that we die as organically as we live. Cremation is a very efficient means of disposal in that what remains is easily disposed of, but concerns have been raised about the levels of mercury and other emissions from crematoria. These are very carefully monitored, however, and at the moment there is very little evidence about the possibly detrimental effects on the surrounding environment. These scares do crop up from time to time and it would be sensible to absorb and analyse the available data so that we can make an informed choice when we need to.

In any case, an organic funeral does tend towards burial. The natural burial centres and woodland burial sites that have been springing up over the last 10 years are a new and different way of giving yourself back to nature. These sites are managed with sensitivity and commitment and many of the funeral requirements can be provided on site. Some carry a limited selection of suitable coffins in eco-friendly materials and the cost is roughly equivalent to the basic package provided by a funeral director.

There are no traditional memorials or headstones. Instead a tree will be planted as a memorial on or close to the site of the grave. Some natural burial centres are situated in beautiful meadows, and wild flowers and bulbs are planted over the grave. The surrounding area will then be left to nature, though managed sensibly, of course, to allow healthy growth and for plant and wild life to flourish.

There is one possible concern that should be mentioned. These sites tend to be privately owned, so there is always the possibility that the site you have chosen may be developed at some later date. Many sites, however, have a covenant attached which will prevent this from happening so, if this is a worry, don't be afraid to ask.

Woodland Burials
With many urban graveyards and cemeteries in this country largely at capacity, and given the reluctance among many people to choose cremation, as a society we are going to have to look for suitable alternative means of disposal if we are to avoid problems for future generations.

Woodland burial sites are now becoming a viable alternative, and in the last 10 years there has been a proliferation of these sites across the country. Although most of these sites are privately owned, there are a number of new civic sites, which opens up the possibility to a wider range of people.

Woodland graves
* the average cost of a private woodland grave is approximately £600, with the council option slightly cheaper at about £500

Choosing a Coffin

This is often regarded as one of the hardest tasks when it comes to arranging a funeral. Not only is there a bewildering choice available to you, but you may also feel anxious about the costs – which can be prohibitive. Another factor is the sense one must choose the 'best' coffin available. This feeling is natural enough, but don't allow yourself to be pressured into selecting a coffin you can't afford.

Your funeral director, if you are using one, will provide a catalogue of what the firm can provide, though if the costs are not clearly displayed, do ask for a price list straight away. This shouldn't be necessary as most reputable funeral directors subscribe to a code of practice that requires them to do this anyway.

Conventional Coffins

The most frequently chosen coffins are constructed from chipboard with a wood veneer, though you can, of course, purchase a solid wood coffin if you prefer. Handles and other coffin furniture are chosen separately, so if you like the handles on one coffin but prefer another coffin itself, then the funeral director will be happy to arrange this for you. All coffins must carry a plaque on which will be engraved the name, age and date of death of the deceased. Crematoria are scrupulously monitored and they insist on this plaque to avoid any possibility of a distressing mix-up.

You do not have to buy a coffin from your funeral director. You can acquire coffins from various other sources, and most funeral directors will accommodate this particular request, either by ordering an alternative for you, or you can arrange to have the coffin you have bought from another source delivered directly to your funeral director.

Biodegradable Coffins

Another option is the biodegradable coffin. These are in fact required by woodland burial sites as MDF and chipboard coffins with a wooden veneer produce some nasty pollutants, such as formaldehyde, and the chemicals released can and will poison the environment. These coffins are made from recycled materials or from materials from renewable sources such as bamboo or willow. Bamboo is a particularly suitable material in that it is fast-growing, therefore easily renewable, and completely pollution-free.

Biodegradable coffins are now widely available in a number of materials. Coffins fashioned from bamboo, wicker and cardboard are among the new options available.

Cardboard coffins are of an extra-thick and very durable 'toughwall' construction, incorporating double-thickness corrugated board with additional lining for support along the base. They have die-cut handles on each side and at each end. The maximum internal size is 183 cm (6 ft 2 in) long and 56 cm (22 in) wide. Cardboard coffins can be decorated with water-based paints and flowers. For those with a belief in protecting the environment, they are the ideal solution for burial or cremation.

There is no loss of dignity, should that issue arise, in these choices. Often families worry that they might be selling their loved one short in some way by using a cardboard or other biodegradable coffin. Old ideas and traditions linger and it is hard to dispel the idea that a grand coffin is the only decent way in which to send a precious family member on their final journey. This is very much a matter of opinion and, if you and/or your loved one do have strong opinions on the environment, what better tribute to him or her than to observe environmental principles in this way.

The Coffin Cover

A coffin cover is a relatively new concept, though there is evidence that there was a similar practice during the Victorian era. The more recent incarnation, though, is designed to appeal to those who have environmental concerns.

The coffin cover arrangement is externally a conventional coffin, which houses a separate internal coffin made of a biodegradable material that is simply removed from the outer shell just prior to burial or cremation. Apart from its obvious green credentials, it also has the advantage of being considerably cheaper than the average coffin. The outer coffin folds flat once the inner coffin has been removed.

The outer cover never comes into contact with the body and can therefore be re-used. There is no question about this being a 'second-hand' coffin. The cost is for the inner coffin, the 'rental' of the outer being included in the price.

Suppliers

There are a number of companies that sell different types of biodegradable coffin:

- Ecopod coffins are made from recycled newspaper, and are decorated with paper made from silk and mulberry leaves. They come with a mattress and an optional feather lining. They are strong and light and can accommodate a person of up to 185 cm (6 ft) tall and up to 95 kg (15 stone) in weight. These coffins are available from Arka.
- Compakta also makes coffins from recycled sources.
- Greenfield Coffins Ltd produces coffins made from 100 per cent biodegradable materials. Their coffins arrive ready assembled and will hold a slightly bigger person than the Ecopod.
- Celtic Caskets supplies a number of environmentally friendly biodegradable coffins. Among their best sellers is the Bamboo coffin.
- Bamboo Eco Coffins are available from Highsted Farm. The bamboo coffin is produced using minimal treatment on the cut bamboo, so no harmful chemicals are involved.
- Green Endings UK Ltd offers a coffin cover service.
- Other companies such as Peace Funerals; Green Undertakings of Watchet; JC Atkinson and Son; Gillman &

Son Funeral Service; The Purple Funeral Company Ltd;
Green Undertakings Ltd.

See Useful Addresses, pages 335–41, for all contact details.

Burial Compared with Cremation

Family members may have strong personal feelings on the
subject and it could be difficult to know which to choose. In
these circumstances, it might be wise to form a sort of
committee to establish whether or not the deceased had any
firm views on either burial or cremation, as well as what each
of those involved feels.

If, after discussion, you still remain undecided, examine the
case for both and see if this will help make your minds up.

Burial

Burial provides a physical point of contact with the deceased –
a place to go and visit, take flowers and commune. Long-term
maintenance might ultimately be a problem, however, not to
mention the fact that the grave is only on leasehold. People
often refer to buying a plot, though this is slightly misleading.
A grave is usually leased to a family, with the cemetery
authority retaining the rights of ownership.

You can buy the exclusive right of burial in a particular plot
for a period, which will not exceed 100 years. This form of
leasehold operates in much the same way as any other. You buy
the right to use the site for the limited period and at the end of
that time, that right as well as the possession of that site will
revert to the original owner.

Prices for grave plots vary enormously across the country
and it is not possible to estimate an average cost. The costs for
urban plots are higher than those in rural areas.

The same principles apply to natural or woodland graves.
The leasehold is potentially shorter as these sites are
individually owned parcels of land, and are therefore subject to
the whims of the landowner. The Natural Burial Centre will
be able to advise you (see Useful Addresses, page 339).

Cremation

A hundred years ago most people were buried. Cremation was still a relatively unusual means of disposal and at the turn of the twentieth century the number of bodies cremated could be counted in hundreds. Long-held beliefs and ideas about the Last Trump or the Day of Judgement encouraged people to feel they might need their bodies again one day, so naturally cremation was regarded with some suspicion. However, opinions changed (very much as a result of the circumstances and scale of deaths during the First World War) and, with the increasing pressure on already restricted space in churchyards and cemeteries, cremation now accounts for about 500,000 disposals a year.

The Federation of British Cremation Authorities (FBCA) is the institution representing all cremation authorities in the United Kingdom. It issues guidelines and directives with regard to cremation, and closely monitors all issues relating to it. Crematoria must operate within the Environmental Protection Act (1990), so the FBCA is particularly concerned with the emissions from crematoria and therefore has been rigorous in enforcing any new health and safety regulations. It has specific requirements for coffin design and prohibits the use of any material (such as PVC or zinc) that might pollute the atmosphere. Anything else placed within the coffin must also be closely scrutinised before cremation takes place as these can also be hazardous; even clothes and shoes in man-made fibres can cause unnecessary smoke and pollution. Although the FBCA does not prohibit the incineration of chipboard and MDF coffins with veneers, these coffins contain high levels of toxic chemicals, including formaldehyde. Their emissions can only contribute to the greenhouse effect, so it is very much in the wider public interest when planning a cremation to opt for a biodegradable coffin if possible.

The other hazard that must be considered is the explosive potential of medical devices such as pacemakers. If you are considering cremation as an option, please let your funeral director know if the deceased has such a medical implant so arrangements can be made for its removal before the funeral. Breast implants are also potentially dangerous, so it might be worth mentioning that as well. It might be possible to remove some artificial joints and/or plates as well, particularly if they can be re-used.

However, most metals – such as jewellery, bolts, screws, metal plates and artificial joints – pass through the cremation process without any difficulty. They form little pieces of aggregate metal, which are removed at the end of the process and disposed of (usually buried in the grounds of the crematorium). Contrary to what some may believe, these little pieces of aggregate are not sold on, nor are they removed from the site.

Other advantages of cremation are that it is cheaper, if finances are a concern, and, once the ashes have been disposed of, there is minimum maintenance, or even none at all. If you should wish to inter the ashes, then a small space will be made available, usually with room for a commemorative plaque and perhaps somewhere to place a small posy of flowers.

The advantages of a service at a crematorium for those who are not particularly religious are as follows:

- a service may take place without any religious element
- you can play the music of your choice
- you can witness the coffin being committed to the cremator, provided the crematorium authorities agree, this would be of particular relevance to those of the Hindu religion
- you may be able to receive the cremated remains on the day of the cremation itself

Finally, because of the nature of crematoria, there may be a feeling that you're in a queue as you await your turn before the funeral, and then face the next group of mourners as you emerge after the service. In order to avoid this sense of being rushed, two cremation times can be booked, though this would of course attract an extra fee. Alternatively, you can choose to have the service in a church, then proceed to the crematorium for the commital.

Disposal of Ashes

While most people still see a religious service as a key part of the process at the time of death, the subsequent disposal of ashes is being considered in increasingly imaginative ways by some families and friends. Some other non-religious groups are actively looking for alternatives. Importantly, the end of a person's life, whether a spouse, partner or friend, will be seen by some as the opportunity to celebrate the wonderful times experienced together and they may want to make the event a happy one.

Ashes can be scattered at a favourite spot or buried at sea and there are now a number of more unusual ways of disposal as well. Usually before cremation, you will be asked what you would like done with the ashes.

If you live at a distance from the crematorium, and are subsequently unable to collect the ashes yourself, most funeral directors will be happy to collect them for you and will hold them until you are ready to collect them in person. Alternatively, they may be able to arrange delivery via courier or, if you live less than 80 km (50 miles) away from their offices, they may be willing to bring them to you themselves. Most crematoria will hold the ashes for you if the funeral director cannot help, though they will charge a small monthly fee for storage. Sending ashes through the post is risky and expensive so it might be better to consider the options already mentioned.

Fees for any of the above services vary enormously, so please make enquiries locally.

Note: When scattering ashes, do be mindful of wind direction. It may be stating the obvious, but on stressful occasions we can sometimes forget to be sensible.

You might like to know that ashes don't necessarily have to be interred, scattered or kept on the mantelpiece. There are some other possibilities now available to you, though some are currently available only in the country of their development (see Useful Addresses, pages 335–41, for all contact details):

- The ashes of Gene Roddenberry, creator of *Star Trek*, were launched into outer space with the help of a company called Celestis Inc., which organises memorial spaceflights. Your ashes can be launched into space for about $5,000 (£2,800).

- LegaSEA is a company that specialises in making bronze and glass memorial urns that double as time capsules. The idea is that you fill the urn with the ashes of your loved one, along with a few of his or her possessions. The capsule is then placed on the ocean bed.

- Eternal Reefs mixes the cremated remains with concrete to form artificial reef modules, which will then be placed on reefs where help is needed. You can visit and dive on these reefs at a later date.

- Eternal Ascent places the cremated remains in a biodegradable balloon, which is then released into the atmosphere. When it eventually fractures into countless tiny pieces, the ashes are dispersed.

- The UK-based company, Heavens Above Fireworks, will pack the ashes of your loved one into fireworks and will then arrange a fabulous farewell display.

- LifeGem can arrange for the cremated remains of your loved one to be turned into diamonds.

Flowers

The funeral director can arrange flowers for the funeral service if you wish. He or she will have a limited selection of arrangements from which you can choose the most suitable. Or you can visit a local florist, who will guide you through the choices available.

If you would like flowers to have a personal touch but do not think you have the know-how, it is always worth talking to the ladies who usually arrange the flowers in church. They would probably be willing to help you and might be able to provide, within reason, season permitting and so on, exactly the kind of arrangements you hope for. They can be immensely talented and very often their expertise is overlooked in favour of the professional flower arranger.

You may not want people to send or bring flowers; it might be your wish to have no flowers or family flowers only and the money that others would have spent on a floral tribute donated to a charity instead. If you decide this, you must make it clear. If you are using a funeral director they will tell anyone who contacts them that this is your wish: if you are arranging the funeral yourself you will need to tell all the people you contact.

Gay and Lesbian Concerns

With regard to the funeral service, there are clergymen who, in spite of the church's stance on gay issues, will be sympathetic to a bereaved person who was in a committed gay relationship. For further assistance, contact the Lesbian and Gay Bereavement Project (see Useful Addresses, page 339), which will be able to put you in touch with someone who can help. You can always go along to see your local parish priest and see which way the land lies; you may not get the answer you want but you should be received with courtesy and understanding.

PLANNING THE
FUNERAL SERVICE

Choosing the Venue

Whether it takes place in a church or a crematorium chapel or even in a woodland glade, the service is a final celebration of someone's life. It is goodbye and can be unbearably sad, but it can also be a celebration of the life of a person whose love and friendship will have enriched the lives of many others. The venue for a funeral is an integral part of that celebration and should be chosen with as much care as everything else to do with the funeral. You may already know the person's wishes. If you do not, then think about what you feel they would most appreciate.

Once you've chosen the venue, you will then have to decide what form the service should take. There are very few rules governing the shape of a funeral service. You can, within reason, do pretty much what you want. You don't have to have a minister of religion present – the possibilities for being independent are endless. Humanist-based ceremonies can be just as uplifting as those in church, so do explore these options if you feel you would like to. The British Humanist Association's contact details can be found in Useful Addresses, page 336.

The Church Service

According to recent research, many people, when asked, preferred the idea of a funeral with some religious input. The church funeral offers just that – and more. The church is still central to many communities, particularly smaller ones. Churches are not only houses of God, they are also places of beauty and serenity and, when one considers the sanctity of human life, it is fitting that someone's last formal occasion should take place in a sacred environment. For some, perhaps, this will not be right, but for many this final blessing conferred on a loved one will not only bring comfort to the bereaved but will also lend the occasion a feeling of rightness – not righteousness, but a sense that it has been well done. The informal formality of a service that has been decided between you and your parish priest with the help of your family, the funeral director and others, will make the final result a personal and meaningful send-off.

Music for the Service

In the final section of this book you will find a wide selection of musical choices if you find you don't have immediate preferences for the right and appropriate music for the service. If possible you should try to choose music you know the deceased loved and would have enjoyed.

If you want a particular organist, you should check that he or she will be available on the day – most organists have day jobs as well – though if not a substitute should be available. The organist will be able to make suggestions about suitable music, if needed, though if you already have ideas about what you would like you should check that he or she is able to play the pieces, and also that compositions not originally written for organ are suitable for the instrument. Do be prepared to be flexible. Most organists will have to be paid for their services.

Alternatively, you might think about engaging a chamber group to play some favourite music, or you may even have a musical friend who is prepared to perform at the funeral.

A widely chosen option is to use CDs. The church may have the facility to play CDs or you may have to make arrangements for this yourself.

If you have chosen something different and less mainstream, you may have to clear it with the minister, but he or she will usually be sympathetic and will permit most things. However, if the deceased had a taste for music with violent or unsavoury lyrics, your request is likely to be tactfully denied.

Choir

Although most churches have a choir, the people who sing in them are not usually professionals, so it is unlikely that many of them would be available mid-week to sing at a funeral. If you feel you would like a choir to sing at the funeral, you could consider the possibility of employing a professional group, or even a soloist. There are small groups available for hire that might fit the bill. Their repertoire may be restricted, though they may also be willing to learn something new, particularly if it is important to you. Fees will vary enormously, so do enquire before rushing into anything. As well as the usual information sources such as the Yellow Pages, your local music shop may have a notice board where such groups advertise, or try the library.

Hymns

Many of us will know a small selection of hymns, probably learned in primary school. The organist or the vicar will be able to guide you if you would like something more pertinent to the occasion. Although this is a sad time, don't just choose mournful hymns – try to include a few uplifting ones too.

Readings for the Service

In the final section of this book there is a comprehensive selection of readings to help you choose. You may, of course, have your own ideas and may enjoy the task of looking out poetry and prose that best reflect the character and personality of the deceased.

The Tribute

Sometimes called a eulogy, a word that has its roots in the Latin word for praise, the tribute is the brief summing up of a person and his or her life. The aim of any tribute should be not only to give a flavour of that person, who they were and what they stood for, but also to praise them for their achievements.

There are several very good publications on the subject, which you may be able to find in your local library or bookshop. The leaflet *Well-Chosen Words: How to Write a Eulogy* is a very useful tool to aid you as you set about writing your tribute. It is available free from Co-operative Funeralcare (see Useful Addresses, page 336).

Many people find the thought of having to write, not to mention deliver, a tribute too overwhelming. They may be exhausted by the recent event, and there may be no other family member willing to take on the task. Some simply do not know how to go about it or where to start. If you fall into this category, do not worry. The minister will probably be able to do it for you, especially if he or she already knew the deceased, but if not all you have to do is provide the important details of the deceased's life and the minister will be able to put together a tribute and deliver it for you. A tribute can also be given by a family member or a friend, or even shared between two or more people.

If you feel up to the challenge yourself, and you would like to say some words, the important thing to remember is that you don't have to worry that you're not Shakespeare. When you speak about someone you have known and loved and you speak from the heart, your words will be the most wonderful tribute to that person. What matters is that the tribute will be yours. Although many ministers can speak for you, and will do so beautifully, without previous knowledge of your loved one something of the special personal touch that love and friendship might bring to a tribute will be lost.

Making a Start
Make a list of information about the person (for simplicity, we'll assume here that the person was male):

- dates – birth, marriage, births of any children, day he started work, day he retired, any other significant dates you can think of
- his wife/partner, children, grandchildren
- his parents, brothers and sisters
- where he was born and brought up
- where he went to live later in life
- where he went to school – any honours and/or brickbats
- work and colleagues
- extra-curricular activity – memberships of clubs, societies, political inclinations
- other achievements – sporting, fundraising, charity work, fabulous cook etc.
- attributes – generosity, kindness, humour, good looks etc.
- his philosophy in life

In addition, ask family and friends for extra anecdotes and memories and make a note of these for possible inclusion.

Getting Going

When you write a tribute, in a way you're writing someone's curriculum vitae. CVs tend to start with the most recent employment and this may be a good starting point for you.

For example, 'If Joe Smith were here today, he could look back over many long and happy years, and congratulate himself on his lovely growing family and a life well-spent. Born in 19XX in Swindon, his parents, Maude and Eric, were immensely proud of their baby boy…', and so on.

The next thing is to look at your list of his life achievements and to amplify them. Include little stories and escapades that remind you of him. Don't just mention the glowing reports either; include a few of the things that went wrong: he wouldn't have been human if everything in his life had been perfect.

Finishing the Tribute

Once you've started, knowing when to stop is equally hard. Be brutal with yourself. Once you have written a first draft, read it out aloud to yourself, timing yourself as you do so. If it takes more than 10 minutes, you've probably said too much. Ask a family member who knew the deceased to listen and comment. Make sure the content is balanced; for example, you may have said too much about his schooldays and not enough about his later life.

You can sum up with something personal – what he meant to you and how much you will miss him.

Make sure the over-riding sense of the tribute is that this person meant something and was important and most of all that he or she will be missed.

Finally
Doing something like this is a big deal if you are not used to speaking in public. But you don't have to learn it off by heart; you can read your tribute from your notes if you wish. Stay calm and read slowly and clearly. When you practise at home, take note of where you have to stop and breathe. Split up your notes into lots of paragraphs, rather than having them in one big block, so that when you look up you can easily find your place again.

The Address

Although this is not essential – after all, someone may be delivering a tribute – you might like the minister to say a few words. It won't be a sermon exactly, rather a few spiritual and comforting thoughts – some words to provoke contemplation of our own time on earth and what we should make of it. He or she will mention the deceased, of course, and will urge us to give thanks for them, and to thank God for their life. If the minister has delivered the tribute on behalf of the family, then he or she may just add a few words after that and dispense with the address altogether. You can discuss this with the minister and let your preferences be known.

Prayers

These can be organised by the minister should you wish, or you or a member of your family could write these and read them out at the service yourselves if you feel up to it. Prayers for the dead and the bereaved will also be said in church on subsequent Sundays, so your loved one will be remembered not just on the day of the funeral itself but later too.

Book of Remembrance

This is an idea from an American friend, and it is something you may wish to consider. You can have it in the church or crematorium chapel for people to write their own messages of condolence or their thoughts about the deceased, either as they arrive or before they leave after the service. It can then be kept as a memento of the day.

Coffin Bearers

Usually, the funeral director will organise this. If you wish family or friends to fulfil this office, then talk to the funeral director about how it should be arranged. Many people find it an honour to be asked to perform this last duty for a family member or friend.

Burial

If you have opted for burial then, after the church service, the coffin will be taken to the place of burial. If you have managed to secure a plot in the churchyard, this is a relatively simple process that will involve the bearers carrying the coffin out to the grave. If you have to travel further afield for the burial, then the usual form is just for the immediate family and perhaps a few close friends to go with the vicar for the committal and burial. Other attendees may adjourn either to the house or an alternative venue for the reception.

The grave will have been prepared and usually the gravediggers will have made the site as presentable as possible by laying green cloths around the exposed edges. The vicar will then say the words of committal and the coffin will be lowered carefully into the grave. The committal is a short blessing made prior to burial or cremation. You will be familiar with some of the words – '...ashes to ashes, dust to dust...' etc.

At this point it is sometimes customary for family members to throw a handful of earth and sometimes flowers on to the coffin. These symbolic gestures represent burial and a final goodbye.

The Crematorium Chapel Service

If the deceased is to be cremated, you have the choice of either having the main service in the church followed by the committal in the crematorium or having the full service in the crematorium chapel. Because of the nature of crematoria, there may be a 'conveyor-belt' factor to think about, and if you are worried that this might bother you, it is possible to book two sessions to avoid the sense of being rushed. This will also give you some leeway with the service – you can add in any extras without the inhibiting and upsetting feeling that the authorities are clock-watching. Generally a church service allows significantly more time.

You can ask the minister of your or the deceased's church to take the service in the chapel at the crematorium. Although much of the information about music, readings and addresses covered in The Church Service above will be relevant to a crematorium service, it is usually more restricted due to the time factor; there might be a couple of hymns plus a few readings, a short tribute, some prayers and usually a brief address – delivered by the minister or a friend or relation – and the committal will take place in the chapel.

After the committal, usually the coffin will then slip away on runners for cremation or curtains will close round it. However, one can also ask for the coffin to stay in place or for the curtains to remain open as everyone leaves, which can alleviate the feeling of finality. This is a personal choice.

The minister in charge will say a prayer of blessing and there may be one more hymn. After this, the congregation will leave.

Some crematoria will have the ashes ready for collection on the day of the funeral, but usually the ashes are picked up by a relative for disposal in the chosen way at a later date.

Please be assured that the container of ashes you are given really will be those of your loved one. The cremation procedure is strictly regulated to prevent any possibility of error.

Making the Final Choices

If there are difficulties in making decisions, you can either, as the next of kin, over-rule the rest of the family and their objections and make the final choice yourself or you can ask a close friend of the deceased to throw the casting vote.

Public Service Funerals

Local authorities and some hospitals will provide free funerals for people who have no relatives. This service is provided mostly for patients in long-term psychiatric care, where perhaps a person has been abandoned and sadly forgotten by his or her family, or where no family survives.

A small plaque or memorial is usually erected to the person's memory.

CHOOSING MEMORIAL STONES AND PLAQUES

Whether you plan to bury or cremate the deceased, you will probably want to erect some kind of memorial to them. You may wish to have a simple, upright headstone, or a flat memorial stone.

After burial, the ground must be allowed to settle for 6–12 months, though the length of time recommended varies from region to region and is dependent on the local soil type. This piece of received wisdom may be debatable as the headstone itself will be situated on undisturbed ground; in some cases you may be allowed to put the stone up relatively quickly, say within 3–6 months, so it is worth asking if you would like the headstone to be erected as soon as possible.

Before you order a memorial stone, be aware that there will be regulations to observe. Check with the relevant authorities what their guidelines are. If there are objections to what you would like or had planned, don't get upset or angry; try to negotiate a solution that will satisfy both parties. No one will deliberately want to thwart you, and if your request is refused it will be for good legal reasons and not arbitrary ones. If you were thinking of something unusual for your headstone, do think about the effect it may have on others – what you see as fitting may cause upset or offence to the families of those buried next to your loved one. You may also have to observe height restrictions for your headstone so, again, do ask what the local guidelines are before going ahead with your order.

If the deceased is being buried in an existing grave, then the headstone will have to be removed. It can be replaced after the requisite settling period. Any stonemason will be able to add the name of the deceased and other wording to a headstone, though, if you can, you should use the stonemason who engraved the stone earlier so the addition matches the original.

If you are burying ashes in a cemetery, there will be space for a small plaque and somewhere to place flowers. If you have scattered the ashes of your loved one, you can also have a memorial plaque, and you may also be allowed to plant a rose bush (for example) in the gardens of remembrance most crematoria have. You will have to maintain it yourself or, for a small fee, the crematorium staff may do it for you.

What Goes on a Headstone or Memorial Plaque?
Not everyone knows what to put on a headstone or a plaque. There are so many variations. Some prefer to keep it simple with just the name of the deceased and his or her dates. Some want to acknowledge that this person was loved and will be missed. If you are uncertain as to what might be best, you could visit a cemetery and have a look at memorial inscriptions there. You may find one that appeals to you and gives you inspiration. Ask your family to help with ideas too.

Another consideration might be Memorials by Artists Ltd, a registered charity owned by the Memorial Arts Charity (see Useful Addresses, page 339). Its website states the following: 'Memorials By Artists is a nationwide service which helps people commission fine, individual memorials for churchyard, cemetery, garden or public space.'

For details of reputable stonemasons, contact the National Association of Memorial Masons (see Useful Addresses, page 339).

Finally....
You could also create a virtual memorial. You can either set up your own web page with photographs and anecdotes and perhaps a guest book for family and friends to add their own thoughts and recollections. Or, if you don't feel you're up to the task yourself, there are a number of online companies that are able to set up a web page for you: www.memory-of.com; www.partingwishes.com; www.withus4ever.com

UNUSUAL REQUESTS

Burial at Sea

Normally the only people who are buried at sea are those who have died at sea, either in action during a war or, more rarely, while travelling. In the latter case, the captain of the ship will try to keep the body in cold storage until the ship reaches the next port. However in exceptional cases, such as death from a virulent disease, the person may well be buried at sea.

For those who have had a seafaring career, the bed of the ocean would seem to be a fitting final resting place. However, be warned that the procedures are fairly complex and extremely expensive. It may be easier and less stressful if the deceased were to be cremated first, as there are no current restrictions on the scattering or burial of ashes at sea. However, if the deceased's last wishes were that his or her body should be buried at sea, then it is possible to find a way through the maze of environmental directives.

You will need to apply to the Sea Fisheries Inspectorate (see Useful Addresses, page 340) in order to get permission, and the funeral director will do this for you. In the normal course of events, all matter to be disposed of at sea will require a licence but, in this case, the Government will accept a letter from the funeral director stating that this is how the family intends to dispose of the body. The letter must have the following information:

- the name and address of the applicant
- a suggested date and time for the burial
- a copy of the Death Certificate
- permission from the coroner to remove the body off-shore (an application on Form 104 will be required and the permission for burial at sea will come on Form 103)

- a declaration as to whether the deceased died of an infectious disease (this may affect the outcome)

There are not many sites around the UK where this kind of burial may take place, but the Sea Fisheries Inspectorate will be able to advise you of the locations. They are all outside the 3-mile limit.

The coffin will have to be constructed from solid wood, have a large number of holes and enough ballast to ensure that it sinks on entry to the water.

Don't forget the boat. You will need to hire a boat big enough to manage the coffin and any members of the family who are to witness the ceremony. The minister should be able to accompany you on your brief voyage for the committal.

Burial in an Existing Grave

In theory a conventional grave will hold more than one person, so it is possible for a married couple as well as perhaps one other member of their family to occupy the same plot, if that is their wish.

If you think that you might want to be buried in the same grave as your spouse, it is important that you consult with your funeral director, as a deeper grave will need to be dug.

Your funeral director will be able to make the necessary arrangements for you.

Burial on Private Land

In theory you do not need permission from anyone other than the land-owner to bury a limited number of individuals on private land.

Planning permission is not required for non-commercial sites in the UK. However, you would be well advised to consult your local office of the Environment Agency to make sure there are no mains water supplies near where you are planning to bury the deceased. There is a minimum distance required that must be observed.

You will, of course, need a Certificate for Burial or Cremation (sometimes called the Green Form), so that if any well-meaning passer-by should happen to see you and report your actions to the police, you will be able to allay any suspicions on production of the certificate.

Burial Outside a Cemetery

Most people are unaware that you can in fact be buried anywhere. Most know about burial at sea and the woodland burial schemes that are becoming more popular, but you can, if you wish and certain formalities are observed, elect to be buried on your own land. You will need the full permission of the local authorities and, if you are tenants, that of the landowners.

You must first have a Certificate for Burial or Cremation from your local Registrar of Births, Marriages and Deaths; or, if the coroner has been involved, his or her office will provide a similar certificate. You may also have to apply to the Home Office Coroners and Burials Team (see Useful Addresses, page 338) for permission.

If you do decide to bury the deceased on your own land, either because it was his or her last wish or because you would like the remains to be close to you, do remember that the property may have to be sold in the future and that a grave in the garden may adversely affect its value. The other point to remember when contemplating this kind of burial is that, if you do have to sell up at any time and are unable to remove the body (exhumation of a body is very expensive), you will not necessarily be able to visit the grave again. The new owners may object.

If you do intend to bury the deceased in the garden, you must notify your local council as it has powers to prevent such a burial for several reasons:

- objections of neighbours

- where the remains might contaminate or pollute the water supply – the remains must be at least 100 metres (330 ft) from any water source

Exhumation

There may be a number of reasons for exhumation, some of which will be enormously distressing for the family of the person whose body is being exhumed. If the exhumation is ordered by the Home Office, then you will not be liable for any of the costs or need to be involved in the logistics.

However, there are other more innocent occasions when exhumation may be on the cards. For example: you may be moving to another part of the country and, rather then travelling regularly back and forth from your previous locality, you may feel it might be easier to move the body of your loved one; you may simply wish to re-inter the ashes of your father in the grave of your mother.

Exhumation costs

Whatever the reason for exhumation, before you consider the possibility, it will be as well to think about the cost if you request such a procedure, which will be considerable

* the exhumation of a body will cost around £10,000.
* the exhumation of ashes will cost from about £70.

As well as being very costly, it is also very time-consuming for the professionals whom you will have to employ for assistance. Government health and safety rules apply in these instances and an official from the Department of the Environment will need to be present. Exhumation cannot take place during normal burial hours, either, which can create even more difficulty for those involved.

For permission to exhume and re-inter a body or cremated remains elsewhere, contact the Home Office Coroners and Burials Team (see Useful Addresses, page 338).

THE DEATH OF
A CHILD

The death of a child is particularly heartbreaking as it goes against the natural order of things and parents who lose a child, in whatever circumstances, are left reeling with a frightening mixture of emotions. Whether a child is stillborn, suffers a sudden infant death, or dies as a result of illness or injury, it is agonising for those left behind.

Thankfully, society is becoming better at understanding and recognising the impact of such a loss on the family and friends, and there are a number of agencies that provide comfort and support – from practical assistance in arranging funerals through to counselling or group therapy. Much of this support will happen or be offered automatically, but it is also important for the bereaved to reach out to those near to them, who will be sure to find ways to help. This will include not only family and friends but also professionals, who may often be able to provide more support as they can do so in a sympathetic but more objective way. This includes:

- doctors and hospital staff
- the family GP
- the parish clergy or members of the local church
- professional bereavement counsellors

Particularly vital issues in these sad circumstances are to find a way to express the many emotions that will be fighting for attention, and to realise the importance of acknowledging the existence of the child as a person in his or her own right. This will be a long and difficult process but there are ways to help it on its course.

- Acknowledge that the world has changed and will not be the same again. That does not mean it cannot be a good place to be in the future.
- Try to let go of the inevitable feelings of guilt; they will only hold back the healing process.
- Do not be too impatient to move on; this will be a long and slow process.
- Use the everyday to help you; simple tasks can be reassuring.
- Give yourself time to rest physically; intense emotion is exhausting.
- Take one day at a time; looking too far into the future is simply too daunting.
- Allow yourself time to grieve.
- Try to find an answer to the question 'why', but you may have to accept that you may never find one.
- Talk to others, both those close to you and professionals, to express your emotions. In particular talk to partners about how you feel and, when you are ready, how you can move on.

Many parents will have other children to care for, which will mean that they have to make an effort to continue with everyday life. Remember that those children will also be suffering in their own way and need their own grief addressed. If you feel unable to cope with that, then you will need to find the strength to ask for help from someone and make sure that help is put in place for your child. Close relatives and friends would be the obvious choice but, if that is not possible, contact your GP, who will know where to find support, or your local DSS.

Stillbirth

A stillborn child is one born after 24 weeks of pregnancy and, although it is very painful and difficult, at present in England and Wales both the birth and the death must be registered within 42 days, in Scotland within 21 days. The registrations of both can be done in a single procedure at your local Registrar of Births, Marriages and Deaths.

The doctor or a certified midwife who was in attendance at the birth can issue a Certificate of Stillbirth. If neither a doctor nor a midwife was present, then one of the parents or another qualified informant can make the declaration on Form 35, available at the Registrar of Births, Marriages and Deaths.

If there are any doubts about the birth – perhaps the child was born alive but died soon after birth (a neonatal death) – then the coroner must be informed. This is ghastly for the parents but essential to establish what went wrong.

The Stillbirth and Neonatal Death Society (SANDS) is a charitable organisation that aims to provide support for parents who have lost their babies in this terribly tragic way. There is a network of support groups round the UK and SANDS will be able to put you in touch with the nearest group. Do contact them for further information (see Useful Addresses, page 340).

Planning a Funeral for a Child

Having to arrange a funeral for your child comes at a time when you least feel able to cope with it; the last thing you will want to do is face the awful reality of what has happened. Nevertheless, it has to be done and it is important to know what you can do and what choices there are available to you.

Usually there will be about a week in which you can take the time to make the funeral as special as you possibly can. Try to think of all the things you would like to do, so that when you look back on it, you will not feel you wish you'd done things differently.

You will have to meet with your funeral director as well as your minister to discuss a suitable date and time for the funeral. The funeral director will be able to liaise directly with the minister if you wish, though it is advisable to do this yourself. It will feel better if the minister is not too much of a stranger on the day.

Requesting a Photograph

When your child has been laid out, you may want to have a photograph. It may seem strange to suggest this, but many bereaved parents say they wish they had asked for a last photograph, but were not aware that it was possible.

Flowers

The funeral director can arrange flowers for the funeral service if you wish. He or she will have a limited selection of arrangements from which you can choose the most suitable. Or you can visit a florist, who will guide you through the choices available. Alternatively, you could arrange the flowers yourself, maybe using blooms that have some significance for you; perhaps your child loved daisies for example, in which case little posies of daisies could have much more meaning than something more extravagant and professional.

Some people hand out little bunches of flowers to people as they arrive. Others ask if guests can bring small bunches of flowers from their own gardens.

If you would like flowers to have a personal touch but do not think you have the know-how, it is always worth talking to the ladies who usually arrange the flowers in church. They would probably be willing to help you and might be able to provide, within reason, season permitting and so on, exactly the kind of arrangements you hope for. They can be very talented and often their expertise is overlooked in favour of the professional flower arranger.

As with any other funeral, you may not want people to send or bring flowers; it might be your wish to have no flowers or family flowers only and the money that others would have spent on a floral tribute donated to a charity instead. If you decide this, you must make it clear. If you are using a funeral director they will tell anyone who contacts them that this is your wish: if you are arranging the funeral yourself you will need to tell all the people you contact.

Book of Remembrance

This is an idea from an American friend, and it is something you may wish to consider. You can have it in the church or crematorium chapel for people to write their own messages of condolence, either as they arrive or just before they leave. It can then be kept as a memento of the day and it can be tremendously comforting to know how your family and friends share your grief.

Where to Have the Service

Many people these days do not have any particular religious attachments, but we still like the idea of these major events taking place in church. People often don't feel properly married, for example, unless the ceremony has taken place under a church roof in the presence of God, and before a clergyman. The same can be said of funerals – and there is enormous solace in the idea that your child, however old he or she may have been, is being taken care of by a higher presence and is in a better place now.

Some will not want a church ceremony. A service of remembrance and thanksgiving for the life of your child can be celebrated at the crematorium chapel or even in your home. The British Humanist Association (see Useful Addresses, page 336) can perform services at the chapel or your home. Most crematoria chapels can remove religious symbols if required. Some do not or will not, but in any case they are usually fairly low-key.

Choosing a Coffin

If your loss has been through stillbirth, your baby should also be given full dignity, and these very sad deaths should have the full funeral rites. Usually these children are buried in small white coffins.

With other child deaths, there are all sorts of caskets and coffins available, from the organic through to the more traditional options. It can be tempting to leave everything, right down to the last detail, to the funeral director, and he or she will of course be prepared to take that burden from you. However, it is most important for parents be involved in at least some of the arrangements, not only to give their child a comfortable resting place, but also for their own peace of mind. In the early days, peace is something you may feel you will never experience again, but when you do look back, the sense that you did all you could have for that last day will help with the sadness and regret.

You may want to place your child's favourite toy, some family photographs or one or two other keepsakes in the coffin. This practice is very common and your funeral director will be able to advise you on what is appropriate.

Service Sheets

You can have the order of service printed professionally, once the funeral has been arranged, with the date and time decided and the hymns, poems, readings and music chosen. You will need to arrange this early on and quite quickly, because once you have given the printers the choices and the layout, they will need time to set it up, get a copy of the proof for you to check and then run off the final copies.

You might like to consider making your own service sheets instead. This is something that any other children you have can help you with. They may be able to choose a photograph of their brother or sister, they can draw pictures and perhaps you could ask then to write something special about their sibling or anything else they may want to say. It is vitally important that other children in the family are given a voice and a means of expressing their sorrow too.

Music

Music, always evocative of special moments in your life, can be chosen to reflect the personality of your little one. You can choose your child's favourite songs and tunes to be played at points during the service. If you need further help, there is a section later on in this book dedicated to helping you find the appropriate music.

If you decide to have hymns, there are some beautiful ones suitable for children. Almost all of us will be familiar with *All Things Bright and Beautiful*, for example.

You might like to think about a small choir or a soloist to sing during the service. Church choirs are usually drawn from the community and, since they are volunteers and may be working, they aren't always available mid-week. However, there are professional choirs and other groups who may be prepared to come and sing. Talk to the organist and find out who and what are available or ask in your library and look for advertisements in your local music shop.

Readings

There is a wide range of readings in Part 3 of this book, chosen specially for these occasions. Some of these may be what you are looking for, or they may prompt a memory of something you once read or found personally comforting. Your minister will be able to help you with any readings from the Bible.

The Tribute

However young your child might have been, it is nevertheless essential to acknowledge his or her having been part of your life. A tribute to that child's presence on earth, and what he or she meant to you and your family, will give that brief life meaning, so do not shrink from the thought of a tribute or feel that people will think it is odd.

You might want to give the tribute yourself, or you might want to ask a family member to do it for you. If you would prefer, you can ask the minister to say a few words. He or she will be used to this and will gladly perform the task for you.

After the Service

After the service, the burial or cremation will take place. If you have opted for burial, then the funeral cortege will process out into the churchyard for the committal and burial. The grave will have been prepared for the final task of committing your child's body. Traditionally, handfuls of earth and flowers may be scattered on top of the coffin.

If you have to travel to a cemetery slightly further away, then you and your family and the coffin bearing the body will return to the funeral cars and travel in convoy to the municipal or other cemetery for burial. The same procedures will apply.

If the service has taken place at a crematorium chapel, then the committal takes place in the chapel before cremation.

When It's Over

When the funeral and the reception are over, you will probably feel completely drained. The organisation of the funeral and all the accompanying arrangements will have occupied you and helped tide you over the first days after the death: there is now time to reflect on what has happened. Do make sure you have plenty of company and, if you feel unable to cope, please do seek help. There is plenty out there: see your GP if you have trouble sleeping; have counselling to talk through your feelings; do accept help from friends and family – they wouldn't offer it if they didn't mean it. Most of all don't ask too much of yourself.

FUNERAL ETIQUETTE AND OTHER RELIGIONS

Funeral etiquette used to be very rigid. These 'rules' were largely established by the Victorians, who loved the formality and ritual of funerals. Many of them still apply today to some degree, though things are much less structured than they were even as little as twenty years ago. Although there is less formality now, when we come together on these sad occasions, we should, nevertheless, respect the dead and the bereaved they have left behind with at least a small observance of these old courtesies.

Suitable Dress

For a formal funeral, you would be expected to dress in black, but for most funerals this is not essential although people do tend to choose muted or dark colours appropriate to a sad occasion. You should be guided by the relatives of the person, as some people now prefer to see a funeral as a celebration of the person's life and a leave-taking and may invite you to wear your normal colours. Obviously, the style of dress should also be appropriate to the sensitivities of the bereaved so is usually fairly smart and modest. Men usually wear a dark suit with a black tie.

Remember that, especially for a burial, you may be on your feet for some time and have to walk through long grass or across uneven territory, so comfortable shoes are a good idea.

Letters of Condolence

Letters of condolence are always difficult to write, even to those we love and know well. However, it is very comforting for those who've been bereaved to have a written acknowledgement of the affection in which their loved one was held, and that someone has cared enough to compose a letter to say how sorry they are. It doesn't have to be long or clever – one sincere and heartfelt line will mean so much to your grieving friends or family.

Flowers

Flowers for the funeral are, these days, mostly the preserve of the family. You might instead be asked to donate the money you would otherwise have spent on flowers to a charity nominated by the family. If in doubt, telephone the funeral director and enquire what the family has requested.

Awkward Family Situations

Sadly, it is not uncommon for family issues to create problems at funerals. It should be possible at times like these to put personal difficulties aside for a few hours in order to honour the dead, so if there have been problems in your family, try to be the peacemaker and find a way to resolve the issues or, at least, find a way round them. The most important thing to remember is that a funeral is the time to help the family and friends of the deceased say farewell and to help them come to terms with their loss. You may have to compromise or even make sacrifices in order to achieve that.

Thank You Letters

You should always try and write to the widow or widower or the family to thank them for including you. If you have not already written, it will be an opportunity for you to express your condolences as well.

A Funeral for Someone of Another Faith

If you are invited by the family to a funeral of someone who practised a religion with which you are unfamiliar, you may be uncertain about any particular customs you should observe.

There are some universal principles that will always apply: your dress should be sober and respectful and entirely appropriate. You should convey your condolences to the family as soon as is polite. Don't be afraid to ask someone knowledgeable about any customs; people are usually delighted to help and guide and will not mind or be offended.

If you are involved in the arrangements for a different faith funeral, the Registrar of Births, Marriages and Deaths or the hospital chaplain will be able to advise of specific funeral directors who deal with religions other than the Church of England. Your local funeral director may also be able to point you in the right direction if unable themselves to help. Most crematoria and municipal cemeteries can also advise regarding the requirements for funerals of all religions.

You can, of course, contact your local synagogue, mosque, chapel or temple for assistance directly and you will be able to find the numbers in the Yellow Pages or telephone directory. We have given some central numbers should it prove difficult to find a local contact (see Useful Addresses, pages 335–41).

The Jewish Religion

Jewish funerals traditionally take place within 48 hours of death (or as soon after that as possible). Specialist funeral directors will know about this and will be able to deal with all the arrangements in the necessary time. The body is placed in an inexpensive wooden coffin with a handful of earth from Israel. Jewish funerals take place in Jewish cemeteries, and the funeral service consists of psalms, eulogies to the deceased, prayers for the repose of the soul and a recital of the Kaddish, a hymn of praise to God. Men attend these occasions with only close women relatives present. The women remain separate from the men. After the funeral a simple meal is offered to the mourners.

The Hindu Religion

The Hindu religion dictates that the deceased must be cremated, as burning signifies the release of the spirit. Because of their belief in reincarnation, Hindus do not see death as an end of any sort, but merely as a stage in the soul's journey to the next incarnation as it travels towards Nirvana, or heaven. Death is a sad occasion of course, but Hindu priests place the emphasis on the route ahead as a cause for celebration as well as regret. The cremation must take place in the presence of family members and crematoria will usually allow a small number of relatives to be present.

After the cremation, the family may have a meal and offer prayers in their home. A priest will visit later to purify the house with incense and special prayers and this marks the beginning of the 13-day period of mourning during which relations and friends visit and offer their condolences.

The Muslim Religion

Muslims usually appoint one person in their locality who can deal with their funeral arrangements. Muslims are not cremated but should be buried in individual graves, with their faces turned to the right facing Mecca. It is preferred that the burial should take place within 24 hours. Although tradition dictates that burial should take place in a plain white shroud with no coffin, the regulations in the UK require the use of a coffin at burial.

Members of the family and friends place a little earth into the grave while reciting a verse from the Qur'an. Graves are raised above ground level and kept simple, with only the name and date of death on a stone. Official mourning lasts for three days and culminates in a banquet to remember the deceased.

The Quaker Religion

Quaker funerals are renowned for their simplicity and are invariably in accordance with the last wishes of the deceased. Burial and cremation are both acceptable. The funeral itself is conducted by one of the elders of the church and is mostly a silent gathering, although those who wish to speak may do so. For further information on Quaker funerals, contact your local meeting house or the Society of Friends (see Useful Addresses, page 340).

The Sikh Religion

Sikhs view death as the separation of the soul from the body and this is seen as the will of God.

Death and its surrounding traditions and conventions follow the teachings of the faith. Sikhs believe that after death the soul moves on to meet the Supreme Soul, God. Death is seen as a time for praising God in accordance with the Rahit Maryada.

After death, ardas (prayers) and lines from the Holy Book are said. Sikh scriptures dictate that relatives should not indulge in wailing and anguished mourning. To help with this, hymns are sung and holy scriptures read continuously for 48 hours, or in stages that must completed within one week.

Men should wear black headscarves while the women wear pale or white scarves at the ceremony.

Cremation is the accepted form of disposal, and after the funeral ceremony, a member of the family traditionally lights the funeral pyre. In Britain however this is not possible so it has become customary for a family member to push the button for the coffin to disappear instead. The ashes of the deceased are often scattered in running water or in the sea (Sikhs do not hold any river as holy) or deposited in a place of sentimental value.

Mourning usually lasts between two and five weeks and on the first anniversary of the death, the family and friends of the deceased gather together for prayers and a meal. This is not seen as a sad event but rather as a celebration of life.

The Buddhist Religion

In Buddhism, the funeral is a relatively unimportant affair because of their belief in reincarnation. Buddhists concentrate all their efforts on the mind of the dying person right up to and at the moment of death. Most Buddhist funerals in the West are simple and very low-key with only members of the family and close friends present. The ceremony itself will often be organised by the family and will include Buddhist readings and tributes to the deceased.

The committal is usually carried out at a simple chapel attached to the cemetery and, although most Buddhists prefer cremation, if burial is chosen then a green funeral will take place.

The Humanist Funeral

Humanists believe in a common humanity and in reason rather than in any specific religion. A Humanist funeral aims to be dignified and to honour the memory of the deceased.

There will be personal tributes and readings, poetry and music – perhaps ones favoured by the deceased – instead of hymns and prayers. A Humanist officiant will lead the ceremony, having first discussed with the family the order of the ceremony, timings and other details. (See Useful Addresses, page 336).

Protestants and Roman Catholics

The Roman Catholic and Protestant rites have some similarities. It is common for a requiem mass to be part of the Catholic funeral rites.

Spiritualist Ceremonies

Spiritualist ceremonies will vary considerably depending on the organisation. The emphasis will be on the fact that the loved one has crossed over to an active life on the other side and that they can continue to have a relationship with this world, which will be a protective and guiding one, not one involving any degree of dependency.

LEGAL AND FINANCIAL MATTERS

Charter for the Bereaved

The Charter for the Bereaved was introduced in 1996 as part of the Government's Citizens Charter initiative. It seeks to 'encourage burial and funeral authorities to become charter members and to adhere to a list of rights which they should also bring to the attention of their clients'.

As more people choose to dispense with the services of funeral directors in favour of arranging their own funerals, it is in everyone's best interests to see that the inexperienced do not fall foul of any law or authority or – worse – get taken for a ride by the unscrupulous few who might be willing to take advantage of the grief-stricken bereaved.

There are also rules in place that allow you to complain if you are unhappy about the service you received from your funeral director. There is no national scheme but, if your funeral director belongs to one of the national associations (the National Association of Funeral Directors or the Society of Allied and Independent Funeral Directors – see Useful Addresses, pages 339 and 340), you will be able to seek some kind of compensation for any grievance you feel you have suffered. If an apology is all you are after, rather than financial compensation, do make your feelings known.

Charter members are working hard to establish good relationships with the newer natural burial sites as well as employing sound environmental principles in the management of the more conventional burial sites.

Pensions, Benefits and Allowances; Wills, Property and Possessions

If there are immediate financial problems, there are various ways in which dependents who suddenly find themselves bereaved can find help:

- a bank loan may be available if the estate funds are to be released within relatively quick time and you can prove that you are the beneficiary
- benefits are also available to help you through the period when you have no access to funds

For the latter option, contact the Department of Work and Pensions or your local Jobcentre Plus or Pension Service office.

Bereavement Payment is a one-off loan of up to £2,000 available for immediate needs. It will have to be repaid after the estate has been settled.

Bereavement Allowance is a weekly benefit payable to a surviving spouse aged over 45 at the death of the deceased and who is without dependent children. This allowance is payable for up to 52 weeks following the death.

The Widowed Parents' Allowance is a weekly benefit for a surviving parent who is bringing up a child or children.

If you are man aged 65 or over or a woman aged 60 or over, when your spouse dies you may be eligible for extra retirement pension based on your spouse's National Insurance contributions.

Booklets GL14 and NP45, available from the Department of Social Security (DSS), give information on these payments and how to go about applying for them.

For further details you can visit the Inland Revenue website at www.inlandrevenue.gov.uk. If you do not have access to a computer, ask a friend who has one to help you or go to a library or internet café to log on. There are plenty of people who can help you find your way, so do not struggle unaided.

Note: If you do intend to make a claim for one of these benefits, don't forget to take the Certificate of Registration of Death with you. There is a claim form on the back of the certificate, which you will have to complete and hand in at your local benefits office.

You will not be eligible for any Bereavement Allowance if:

- you are divorced from or were never married to the deceased
- you have remarried or live with someone as if you were married
- you are in prison or are being held in custody

There are limited other options available to you. You might be able to get industrial death benefit if your spouse died as a result of an industrial accident. Ask for details at your local DSS office.

Pensions and Insurance

You can check with your late spouse's employers for details of their pension scheme, if he or she was contributing to one, and who the trustees of the fund might be. You will have to ask these people if you are entitled to benefit from the scheme.

Life insurance, usually taken out in favour of the remaining partner and/or children, may provide payment directly to you if it was written in trust. Otherwise any other payments will count as being part of the estate and will therefore be subject to inheritance tax. It will also be paid out only once probate or letters of administration have been granted.

Car Insurance

If the car insurance policy is in the name of the deceased, then this means that no one else may drive the car until the existing policy is amended. If there are no other drivers named in the policy, but the policy allows for others to drive with the policy-holder's permission, then that permission ceases on the death of the policy-holder. If you are not sure if any of these apply to you, you should ring the insurance company as soon as possible and make new arrangements straight away. They will issue an emergency cover note while the old policy is being amended.

Home and Contents Insurance Policy
Informing the insurance company of your change of circumstances must be done as soon as possible as the policy may lapse if the policy-holder dies. Not all policies have this caveat but do ring and check and, if this is the case, arrange new cover as soon as possible.

Bank and Building Society Accounts

As soon as someone dies, if you find that you are the person responsible for their estate – either because you are the remaining partner, or a relative of the deceased, or are acting on behalf of the partner of the deceased – you must, of course, begin to inform the financial institutions where the deceased may have held accounts, credit cards and mortgages, that the person has died. You will be asked to submit a copy of the Death Certificate as proof and, once you have filled in a number of forms, the banks and building societies will initiate the necessary procedures.

When a bank or building society is informed of a customer's death, normally this information is checked against all possible accounts that he or she might have had with the group, including its mortgage and credit card operations. You should receive an acknowledgement from them and confirmation that these procedures have been put in motion.

Occasionally a bank or a building society can trip up and, although you may have sent them a copy of the Death Certificate, letters addressed to the deceased may continue to arrive. This can be terribly distressing but fortunately, in most cases, this can be rectified very swiftly. If you do encounter this problem with the deceased's bank, do not hesitate to make strong representations, if necessary at the highest level. This kind of mistake is inexcusable.

Personal Bank Accounts

Personal bank accounts are frozen on death. You can continue to use a joint account provided that both signatures are not required on every cheque.

Funeral Expenses from the Deceased's Accounts

Most banks will allow a small cash withdrawal, provided funds are available, in order to help tide the family over the first few weeks, particularly as there will be so much to pay for. You should contact your bank to confirm the arrangements and not try to use their cashcard, even if you know the number, without prior authorisation. After the funeral has taken place, again providing there are funds in the account, the bank will usually pay a funeral director's final bill from the account.

Debts

If you find yourself in the position of having to sort out the estate of someone who was in debt, there are certain procedures you will have to follow and you should ask the solicitor for advice. If you know the creditors, you will be able to get in touch with them. If you do not, you may have to advertise that the person has died, advising any creditors to come forward with their accounts.

You will then have to list the amounts due – mortgages, credit and store cards, utility bills and hire purchase debts, plus the cost of the funeral – and balance them against the value of the house, its contents, cars, and anything else that can be sold. However, there may be life insurance policies that could be cashed in and you may be able to reclaim some money on the TV licence, road tax and car, house and contents insurance.

Wills

The legal terminology of wills can be confusing – archaic and incomprehensible language is used – and, if there is an official reading of a will, you could feel that the solicitor might as well have been speaking a foreign language for all you have understood of what's been said. The solicitor should explain in simple and straightforward English exactly what the will means and who is to have what.

Disputing/Challenging a Will

If you wish to challenge a will, there is a time limit of six months from the person's death.

Sometimes people have what used to be called 'expectations'. For example, a person might believe, rightly or wrongly, that when their parents die, they will inherit their money and property. In most cases, they will indeed inherit the estates of their parents, but just occasionally things don't work out as they had hoped.

As more couples divorce and remarry than ever before, the inheritance problem becomes increasingly complex and fraught. A new much-younger wife may inherit an entire estate from her husband, for example, while the children of his earlier marriage(s) are left with nothing, when they might have expected at least some provision. It can prompt years of wrangling, much bitterness and the only people who really benefit from it are the lawyers.

Occasionally a friend, a former employee or perhaps a carer will claim that he or she was promised something, perhaps a picture or a small sum of money. If the deceased did not mention this in their will, then there is no proof and therefore no onus on the recipients of the estate to recognise this claim. Of course if it was known that the deceased wanted their kind neighbour to have their collection of porcelain thimbles or their compilation of jazz vinyls, then hopefully the gift would be made freely and with pleasure by the family.

You are allowed to challenge a will, if you wish, but bear in mind that it could be expensive and also that it may not make any difference whatsoever to the outcome. If you do decide to make a challenge, you should do so to the solicitor who is holding the will. It may be worth asking your own solicitor for advice on how to go about it.

Mental Incapacity

A will is valid only if the testator (the person making the will) knew and understood what they intended at the time they made their will. If that person subsequently became mentally ill or senile, the will still remains valid.

If a person who was mentally ill or suffering from a psychiatric condition made a will, provided it had been made clear that they knew or understood what they were doing at the time, then it will be agreed that the will is valid.

If you think there are grounds for suspicion, do voice your fears. If, for example, your elderly relative who was known to be senile changed his or her will in favour of a new carer, you do have the right to challenge the validity of the will.

Invalid Wills

A will is invalid if:

- it has not been properly formatted
- it has not been witnessed
- it can be proved that the deceased was not of sound mind at the time when it was made

In addition, a will can be overturned if:

- it can be proved that the person who made the will was coerced in some way into making unexpected changes or a new will
- if it can be proved if the will is a forgery; this is very rare but it does occasionally happen

Note: In all cases where a will might be regarded as invalid, or where it might be open to challenge, you should take legal advice.

Revocation of Wills

Occasionally a will may have been revoked by the testator (the person who made the will) either because he or she made a later will or destroyed the existing one. Also, in certain circumstances the law regards a will as having been automatically revoked:

- By divorce. If the testator divorced after the will had been made, then that will is partially revoked; the will remains valid but any bequests to the former partner are automatically deleted. However, separation without divorce will have no effect on the will and it remains valid.
- By marriage. If a person made a will in favour of a nephew, for example, and then afterwards he or she married, the pre-existing will is revoked.

Usually later wills will state that any former wills are no longer valid. However, if a later will does not expressly revoke all former wills and an executor is left confused by apparently conflicting last wishes, the exectuor can usually make a judgement based on implication. The last (that is, the latest) 'Last Will and Testament' is usually assumed to be the valid one. If the two wills are consistent with each other then they can both be administered. For example, a later will may have added a few bequests, perhaps to carers who made the last few months of the person's life more comfortable.

Bequests

A bequest is anything that has been bequeathed, in other words, the passing on of possessions or money from the deceased to a person or persons named in their will. For instance, a man may bequeath all his worldly goods to his wife upon his death, but may also make a few small bequests to friends and colleagues.

If the deceased had already made a will but decided at a later date that they wanted to make a few additions this may have been done by addition to the existing will in the form of a codicil. The codicil must have been written in the right way and duly witnessed and signed for validity.

Probate

Probate is a legal process designed to ensure that the deceased's money and property is all accounted for, duly taxed and distributed according to their wishes. It also ensures fair play.

The person who applies for probate will usually be a family representative, or an executor (a woman may be referred to as an executrix) or trustee of the will. He or she will have to make a list of the money, property and investments of the deceased and place against them a reasonable value. Even if the estate is relatively modest, it might nevertheless be helpful to ask someone from an auction house to assess the goods and chattels for you, and an estate agent to estimate the value of the house and any other property. If there were investments, then the deceased's broker should also be able to give you a breakdown of their current worth. If the deceased's finances are complex, it might also be worth employing the services of an accountant. He or she will be able to advise you on inheritance tax and may even be able to make savings for you.

The procedure for applying for probate is fairly straightforward and self-explanatory, but if you need guidance the Probate Application Department will be able to help you with any queries (see Useful Addresses, page 340).

You will have to fill in some forms:
- Probate Application Form PA 1
- Account of the Estate

You will then have to be interviewed by an official from the probate registry to complete the formalities.

Probate cannot be granted until after payment of tax, though if items and property need to be sold in order to cover the tax, you may be granted probate after paying part of the full amount.

Letters of Administration

You will need these if no will exists or if no executors have been appointed. The procedures for obtaining letters of administration are the same as for applying for probate.

Inheritance Tax

Inheritance tax is the amount you are allowed to inherit tax-free. The threshold is increased annually.

How inheritance tax is calculated

In the tax year 2005–6, the inheritance tax threshold is £275,000. (Recent Land Registry figures suggest that if the inheritance tax threshold had increased in line with property prices, then it would now stand at £513,850!)

On estates that are valued at up to or less than £5,000, there are no charges to pay. If the estate is valued at up to or less than the current inheritance tax threshold, the heirs are not liable for any tax but they will have to pay a probate fee, currently £130.

If the estate is valued at more than the threshold, the heirs pay 40 per cent on the remaining monies. For example:

* the probate value of the estate = £500,000
* the inheritance tax allowance = £275,000
* leaving £225,000, which is taxable at 40 per cent
* therefore the tax bill will be £90,0000
* leaving the heirs with a total of £410,000

The Estate

For clarification, a person's estate includes:

- Gifts of money or property not covered by any exemption made less than seven years before the death.
- The total value of everything owned in the deceased's name, less bills, funeral expenses and mortgages owing at the time of death.

- The share of anything jointly owned, less the deceased's share of joint bills and mortgages owing at the time of death.
- The capital value of trust funds from which the deceased received some benefit. For example, income received as a 'life-tenant' under the trust or if he or she had the right to live in a house.

There are potential liabilities for gifts of money or property made within 7 years of death. The sliding scale begins with 20 per cent on gifts made 6–7 years before death and increases to 40 per cent on 5–6 years, 60 per cent on 4–5 years, 80 per cent on 3–4 years and 100 per cent on anything up to 3 years prior to death. So, provided the deceased survived for three years after making the gift, it will have benefited the recipient.

Gifts with Reservations

With effect from April 2005, rules were introduced to prevent the avoidance of inheritance tax rules for 'gifts with reservations'. This is a term coined to describe the gift of property or other assets to another party while continuing to enjoy the benefits of them. For example, if the deceased gave the house to another member of the family but continued to live in it, there will be an income tax charge on the benefit gained from using it. How the liability is calculated will depend on the value of the assets. For further information, contact your local Inland Revenue office.

Exemptions from Inheritance Tax

There are regrettably few of these, but what remain are listed below.
- there will be no tax on the assets and property left to the spouse of the deceased
- there will be no tax on assets and property left to charity
- there will be no tax on assets and property left to the heirs of a member of the armed forces killed in action

There are also tax reliefs, though not complete exemption, that reduce the value of qualifying property, for example business assets and farmland.

For further information, see leaflet HT17 from your local tax office.

Intestacy

In the absence of a will, for a family with children, the intestacy rules provide for the surviving spouse or partner:

- a statutory legacy
- the personal chattels
- a life interest in one half of the residue of the estate

Any children are entitled to the other half of the residue once they reach the age of 18.

If there are no children, the statutory legacy for the surviving spouse increases.

2005–6 intestacy rates

* the statutory legacy to a spouse with children is £125,000
* statutory legacy to a spouse with no children is £200,000

A spouse, that is the person to whom the deceased was married even if they were separated or estranged, can nevertheless inherit a share of the estate under intestacy rules. A divorced husband or wife cannot inherit under intestacy rules.

A co-habitee cannot inherit the estate under intestacy rules, though he or she may be entitled as a dependent. You may have to apply through the courts for this entitlement but you must do so within a six-month time frame.

Children, under intestacy rules, are defined as:

- legitimate children of the deceased
- illegitimate children of the deceased

- children adopted by the deceased

Step-children are not regarded as children of the deceased under intestacy rules.

Other circumstances lead to different allocations. If a person dies without a spouse or children, then the legal rights to their property would go, in order, to:

- their parents
- their brothers and sisters
- their half-brothers and half-sisters
- their grandparents

The authorities that deal with these matters will work through any remaining family in order. So, after exhausting the primary family, any aunts, uncles, cousins etc. may claim the allowance, provided there are no closer living relatives. If, after the award has been made to, say, a cousin, a long-lost son of the deceased turns up, then the cousin would probably have to forfeit the inheritance.

If there are no surviving relatives, the estate will pass to the Crown.

Co-habitees

With regard to home ownership, if you were not married to the deceased then you will be treated less favourably. If your home was not jointly owned, you will not be able to claim any share in it unless you are able to prove that you contributed to its acquisition and/or improvement.

If you were co-habiting in a rented property then you must check with your landlord to make sure that he or she is happy for you to continue living in the property and is prepared to take you on as the new tenant.

Rights of succession are granted to protect tenants under the Rent Act 1977. These rights are granted to:

- the spouse of the deceased
- a partner with whom the deceased was living as man and wife, or a partner with whom the deceased was living in a long-standing same-sex relationship

- members of the deceased's family who were living with him or her for at least 2 years before the death

Minors

The surviving parent will usually assume the role of sole guardian of an under-age child or children.

If there is no surviving parent, it is to be hoped that the deceased made arrangements for a trusted friend or relative to become the children's legal guardian. This person should be over the age of 18 and should have been asked by the deceased, to ensure that they were willing to assume the responsibility.

If a child is left orphaned and no guardian is named, then the child will temporarily be made a ward of court, and then any relatives may apply for custody. Custody is usually granted to close relatives such as grandparents or aunts and uncles. However, if no one comes forward, then the child will be put into the care of the local authority, which will then follow the usual routines for fostering and, hopefully, eventual adoption.

Gay and Lesbian Concerns

This is still an area that can be fraught with difficulty, though generally speaking most people are more sympathetic and tolerant than before. Attitudes to same-sex partnerships have changed and these relationships are now much more widely accepted. Most important of all, it is realised that the loss of a same-sex partner is no less devastating.

The law on inheritance tax has finally been addressed with regard to same-sex partners and, when new legislation comes into force in December 2005, the law will cease to discriminate against those who are gay and lesbian and their partners. They will have the opportunity to have their relationships legally recognised under the Civil Partnerships Act. If they decide to sign up to the partnership register, they will receive equal rights with married couples on pensions and inheritance tax. In the meantime, unless your partner made a will stating clearly that he or she wished to make you the beneficiary of any assets, regrettably you have no inherency rights.

If you and your partner were co-habiting in a council house, and you were not the tenant, you may not necessarily inherit the tenancy rights. Check with your local authority; usually there will be no problem whatsoever, particularly if you had been co-habiting for more than two years.

Junk Mail and Unwanted Phone Calls

The Bereavement Register is a free service that has been introduced to prevent junk mail from being addressed and sent to someone who has died. It can be very upsetting for bereaved families to receive this kind of unwanted mail and, once you have registered your details, the volume of mail should start to fall within 4–6 weeks and will have stopped altogether after 6 months. Your funeral director will have a form you can fill in for this service, or see Useful Addresses, page 336, for contact details.

The Bereavement Register also provides a service called Call Guardian, which prevents unwanted telephone sales calls.

British Telecom offers a free service to prevent telephone sales calls, the Telephone Preference Service (see Useful Addresses, page 341).

Silent Call Guard is a service that will prevent those unsettling silent calls that are usually caused by telesales companies whose computers mass-dial for maximum hits (see Useful Addresses, page 340).

The Armed Forces Compensation Scheme

New arrangements have been introduced to compensate for injury, illness or death caused by service in the armed forces after 6 April 2005. The new Armed Forces Compensation Scheme (AFCS) replaces the War Pension Scheme and attributable benefits paid under the existing Armed Forces Pension Scheme. However these will continue to be available where an injury, illness or death was caused by service before this date. The new AFCS will provide for the first time a single compensation scheme covering all members and former members of the armed forces.

For further information contact the Veterans Agency (see Useful Addresses, page 341).

THE JOURNEY
THROUGH GRIEF

The death of someone we love or someone close to us can shatter the foundations of our world and leave us feeling vulnerable and insecure. The shape of our life has changed and we wonder whether we will even be able to put ourselves back together again. Grief is part of life and is a normal and natural reaction to loss. It is something that sooner or later most of us have to go through. It may turn out to be one of the most painful experiences we ever have to undergo.

When someone dies, it turns our world upside-down, our lives out of balance, and our grief can feel totally overwhelming. All the familiar routines we have been used to and assumptions we have made about the future have to be re-evaluated. Unexpectedly we may have to redefine our lives and create new meaning for them. We have to find ways to survive the experience and to adjust creatively to a new situation. It may not be easy.

Although we will often see dead people on television or film, the actual death of someone close to us can be a terrible shock. In previous generations, death usually happened at home and was more openly acknowledged and visible. In our society, death is often far from our sight, hidden from us in hospitals and nursing homes. We are not likely to have thought much about it and therefore feel unprepared for it. Indeed, we find it hard to imagine the loss of our loved ones and we can never anticipate how their death will affect us.

The intensity of emotion that accompanies the death of a loved one may surprise us and leave us devastated. Each death we have to face is different and there can be no rehearsal of the grief it brings. However, as we look back on our lives, we may recognise that we have had other, lesser experiences of loss and feelings of grief. It might have been the loss of something we wanted very much, the loss of a job, the death of a relationship, the loss of physical control or mental ability or the collapse of a dream. These also will have been times of emotional upheaval and change – 'little deaths', in effect. In confronting the death of a loved one, we may be aware of similar feelings and also draw on the supports and strengths that helped us through the pain of loss on previous occasions.

It is very important to emphasise that there is no right way to grieve. It is a journey each of us makes for ourselves, in our own way and at our own pace. There are no short cuts and it can sometimes feel very lonely. Others can help us and walk with us, but nobody can make the journey on our behalf. It can be long and painful.

On the journey through grief there are some general steps and familiar landmarks that are recognisable to those who have travelled the way before. They are different phases that grieving people go through and more is said about them below. Everybody is different and these phases do not have to be experienced in the order they are given. Indeed, the dominant feelings that are part of each phase may be present to a greater or lesser degree throughout the journey through grief.

Knowing how to grieve and something about the stages can be helpful. It can be reassuring to know that the way we are feeling and reacting is normal and not exceptional. We need to be reminded that there are no fast solutions, easy answers or quick fixes that will magic away the pain and sorrow. It is best if we take the stages as they come and look forward to the day when we shall come to the end of the journey through grief.

It can come to an end. People do recover. The pain of loss does dissolve. We can grieve and recover and restore our lives. Some people end up feeling that they have grown stronger through it; in making the journey, they feel they have been taught something valuable and new, something they would never have known had they not travelled that way. However, it is hard work. It takes courage and it takes time – rarely weeks, usually months, sometimes years. It is not uncommon for people to think they have finished grieving long before they are really ready. Other people can certainly think you are over the loss much quicker than you are. There is truth in the saying that time heals. We need time, though we are also aware of another pressure which is to feel 'normal' again and get back to our work, to our familiar routines, to reassure ourselves that life can go on. In wanting to do so, however, we must be careful not to deny or suppress the painful feelings we have in the hope that they will go away. It is important to acknowledge our sadness, confront grief and be attentive to the mixed and often conflicting emotions that we experience.

The Stages of Grief

Grief is a deeply personal experience that affects both our emotional and our physical condition. There are no rules about grieving to which we have rigidly to conform. Nevertheless, there are certain responses and feelings that are commonly part of the process. Sometimes these are mixed together in a whirlpool of emotions that come and go.

Numbness and Shock

Our initial response may be one of shock. We find it hard to believe what has happened. We can be speechless, quite unable to take in what has happened. It does not seem real or possible but more like a bad dream from which we will awake. We may feel quite unable to cry or express any emotion. There may be no feeling at all but just a deadness and feeling of distance from the whole event. It may feel as though this is not happening to us or as though the dead person has just gone away for a while and we expect them to return. Sometimes feelings of panic may invade our dream-like state.

Denial

With shock and disbelief will frequently go denial of the death. The finality of the loss and separation is too much to bear and we cannot accept it. We want to believe it is a mistake, that the loved one is not dead. As a result, we may find ourselves searching for the loved one, anticipating that they will appear again. It is often during this phase that we have an experience of seeing the dead person, sensing their presence, hearing their voice or even feeling their touch.

Anger

As the shock wears off, the impact of our loss starts to sink in and we begin to feel the pain. This may initially be felt and expressed through powerful feelings of anger. Sometimes it can feel quite uncontrollable and overwhelming. We may find ourselves feeling angry towards doctors, nurses, God or others trying to help us. Our family, friends and relatives may be the recipients of our anger. We can feel full of guilt for reacting in the way we do towards them. We may also resent anybody who has not suffered a similar loss and experience. We may feel anger towards the person who has died for leaving and abandoning us. We may question why this has happened and who is responsible. The anger may also be directed at ourselves and can result in negative, destructive feelings that are damaging to our health.

Anguish

When the loss begins to hit us the pain can be immense. This is the time when we feel totally crushed by emotion, vulnerable and fragile. We may collapse in a heap of uncontrollable tears. Suddenly we feel very isolated and alone. We feel drained and bewildered. We feel as though our life has been broken in pieces. We feel a frightening gap that we assume nobody or nothing else can fill.

Depression and Withdrawal

A great outpouring of emotion may be followed by a time of detachment and depression. Feeling very low, we wonder what the purpose is of carrying on. We feel drained of energy. Most activities seem meaningless. We may wish for company and closeness but we also want to be alone, to have space. We may even feel suicidal, thinking that such an act would unite us with the one we have lost. It is a distressing time as we sink into a deep hole and wonder whether we will ever get out or even want to do so.

Guilt

Feelings of guilt often accompany the loss of a loved one. This is a normal part of the landscape on the journey through grief.

- We may feel guilty for not feeling sad or responding in the way others expect. However, when the loved one has had a long and fulfilling life, a good death and we have had a chance to say goodbye, there may not be a strong sense of sadness and loss. We may feel pleased or relieved.
- We may feel guilty about letting go of the loved one because, by doing so, we feel we are abandoning them.
- We may feel guilty for not being present when the person died; that if we had been there we could have prevented it.
- We may feel that we could and should have done more to keep them alive; that we have let them down; that we are responsible for their death. There is a host of 'if onlys' that go through our mind.
- Perhaps the greatest cause of guilt is 'unfinished business' – the feeling that we wish we had said or done something or acted differently and that now it is too late. We wish we could turn back the clock. It is particularly hard when we regret quarrels or negative feelings that were unresolved.

To enable our recovery to take place and our journey through grief to continue, we have to come to terms with our guilt. This will mean getting our feelings out into the open, and forgiving ourselves and others. Guilt is often the place where we become stuck in the grieving process.

Recovery

When we are at the beginning of our journey through grief and overcome by our loss, we wonder whether we will ever recover and cope with life again. There is often real doubt that we shall ever get better. 'Who would have thought my shrivelled heart could ever recover greenness?', asked the poet George Herbert. Well, it is possible. The reality is that most people do recover from grief, reconnect with life and re-invest in the future. It is very important to remember that grief does not last for ever. Recovery, however, is a gradual process. It takes time and is helped by the encouragement of others and sometimes professional help.

The signs that we are on the road to recovery are many.

- We are on the way when we can accept our loss not just with our head but with our heart. Acceptance of the finality of our loss with a realisation that we cannot bring our loved one back helps us to move on. We know that we cannot return to the past. Life will never be the same.
- We find that our sorrow is less intense, that we are able to cope better with our feelings and take more interest in the world. Whereas early on we might have wanted few people around, we are now able to face others more easily. We feel more in the mainstream of life than out on its edge, or submerged at its centre.
- An improvement may be felt in our physical health.
- As we recover, we will live less in the past, take responsibility for our lives and look ahead with hope.
- We are no longer the passive recipients or victims of an overbearing sadness but participants in a new but different future. We feel that life is worth living and may take up new interests of hobbies without feeling guilty. Setting ourselves both short- and long-term goals can be a help in planning for the future.

- We will be near the end of our journey if we can think about our loved one without pain or anguish and even feel that making the journey through grief has helped us to grow and mature.
- There may be a feeling that the support and kindness we have received has been a gift. We have lost much but we have also gained a great deal that we would never have experienced had we not made the journey. It is like emerging into the light from a dark tunnel, like sunshine after cloud, like the dawn after the darkness.
- Gratitude and laughter are dominant over sadness and anger. A transformation has taken place.

Recovery doesn't always happen automatically. We have a part to play and it can be hard work. We must believe it is possible and also want to get there. We need to be willing to let go of our pain and accept that life will be different without our loved one. If we are unable to keep moving and finally be reconciled to our loss, we may find that we become stuck on our journey. Our grieving may then belong to what we call 'unsuccessful' or 'abnormal' grief (see pages 148–9).

Physical Symptoms

The emotional pain of grief can affect our physical and mental health, especially in the short term. Many who have lost a loved one will speak of being 'heartbroken'. Some of the effects of grief may include:

- a tightness in the throat or chest; shortness of breath
- an empty feeling in the stomach
- muscle weakness
- shivering; palpitations; diarrhoea; numbness
- insomnia – staying awake at night thinking about the lost person; the inability to rest except for short periods
- loss of appetite; loss of weight
- headaches
- heightened sensitivity to noise

Psychological Symptoms

It is common to experience some of these intense feelings after suffering a bereavement:

- feeling lost and bewildered
- fear of not being able to cope
- inability to concentrate
- fear of going mad or becoming strange
- a sense that nothing is worth doing any more
- a sense of being disconnected from the world and others – 'an invisible blanket between the world and me' (C.S. Lewis)
- feeling detached from one's own body
- feeling like an automaton
- emotional deadness
- suicidal feelings
- loss of self-esteem

Unsuccessful or Abnormal Grief

As each person makes his or her own personal journey through grief, the distinction between what is normal and what is abnormal is not clear-cut. The following would give indications that the process is in difficulties:

- Anger so severe and constant it dominates the whole of life.
- Clinging on to objects associated with or possessions of the dead person for a very long time. Refusing to move or adjust anything. Going back obsessively to places they frequented.
- Denial. Inability to accept that death has happened and the relationship is over. Talking about the person as though they were still alive.
- Feeling 'stuck' and that the degree of distress is not changing in any way.
- Finding it hard to express feelings and a sense of these feelings being 'blocked'.
- Taking on symptoms of illness of the deceased.

- Personality changes, becoming unusually and increasingly withdrawn and isolated.
- Reliance on drink or medication to get through each day.
- Finding that another difficult situation or loss affects us more than it should. This may be a sign of unresolved grief from earlier loss.
- Excessive grieving – constantly breaking down emotionally.
- Failing to redefine goals and reinvest in the future.
- Holding on to guilt – being unable to forgive yourself for what you said or did.
- Idealising the deceased and failing to be realistic about their strengths and weaknesses.
- Continuing melancholy or depression.
- Fear of death in any form or fear of social interaction.
- Physical illnesses with no obvious medical cause. This may be related to unresolved grief and therefore psychosomatic.

Unresolved grief is very often the result of keeping our feelings bottled up. Of course, some people find it easier to express their feelings than others. That may depend on many factors, including our personality and upbringing. However, restraint is generally not healthy when our lives are knocked out of shape by loss. By keeping it all private or forcing ourselves to be brave, we may put a heavy demand on our emotional or psychological health. Delaying grief to be strong at the time may feel right and be necessary but it will not help to deny our feelings indefinitely. The feelings about our loss are likely to surface in some way later on in life or we shall go on mourning for years after the event.

In order to resolve grief we may have to go back to the event of our loss and experience again the feelings around it. Or, we may need to revisit the place where we got stuck on our journey and go on from that point. This process can take time and may cause us distress and it is unlikely we can do it alone. Professional help will probably be needed (see pages 153–4).

Other Factors in Coping with Grief

There are certain circumstances when grief is more likely to cause problems, in particular when:

- the death has been sudden or unexpected
- the body has not been found
- the death is by murder or suicide
- the body has been mutilated

Our ability to cope with grief may also be affected by our general health, our personality type and external factors. Personalities who are more at risk from abnormal grieving are:

- those who feel unworthy and have low self-esteem
- those who are unable to express their feelings
- those who have had previous problems over loss

The support we have from others on our journey through grief can be significant in helping us to complete that journey successfully. Those more at risk, therefore, include:

- those whose family is unsupportive
- those who have no supportive family network
- those who see no future for themselves

Grief and Memories

There will be times when deep feelings that we thought were passed well up inside us again. They bring back memories that can be both sad and happy. There can be after-shocks to grief. These are likely to happen at special times such as birthdays, anniversaries and Christmas. We will have other experiences when tears come because we wish our loved one could be present to share them. Something another person says or items that remind us of our loss may also revive our grief. We should accept these feelings as normal and natural.

Grief and Love

Some people feel that if they stop grieving they stop loving or that they are letting the loved one down by ceasing to feel sad. They may also be fearful that they will forget him or her if they stop grieving. The strength of our love, however, can never be measured by the depth of our sorrow. Very often the opposite happens; when we let a loved one go, we can see more clearly that he or she will never really be lost to us but will live on in our hearts and memories in a new way.

Grief and Spirituality
The death of a loved one can raise a lot of questions for us about the purpose of suffering, the meaning of life and what happens after death. Sometimes a death will cause us to re-examine the values we live by and what matters to us. It can change our outlook and perspective on life. Grief can be a time of real heart-searching for us. It may bring us face to face with the certainty of our own death.

Our beliefs can affect how we mourn and some will find comfort in their religious faith. People of different cultures and faiths will deal with death in different ways. While everyone has to come to terms with the fact that death is a final farewell in this life, some will be sustained by their belief that death is not the end of everything but the beginning of something new in the closer presence of God.

Anticipatory Grief
We cannot know for certain how we will react or feel when the moment of death comes to a loved one. However, when the process of dying is lengthy and we are expecting death, we can find ourselves already expressing feelings of grief in anticipation of the event. This is both healthy and normal and, as a result, we may already have travelled some way on the journey through grief by the time the death occurs. A word of warning, though, not to assume that, because we have shed buckets of tears before the death, there will not be more to come!

Children and Grief
Children and teenagers also experience grief. They too need to make the journey, go through the phases, be allowed to share

in the sorrow, express their sadness and ask questions. The following are a few guidelines.

- Children of different ages will experience and understand death in different ways. However, they should not be protected or shut out from the feelings surrounding the death. Telling them to 'be brave' may inhibit their need to grieve.

- It is best to be open and honest with children, to be direct and simple when telling them about a death. They may need help to express their feelings and attempting to protect them from reality, even with the best possible intentions, will not be constructive. In any case, children are usually very aware that things are being kept from them.

- Children do not stay with sadness as long as adults and tend to go through the phases more quickly. But they still need time and permission to grieve, with a great deal of love and support.

- Children can get stuck on the journey of grief just like adults. If this happens they may need professional help to move on. Signs that not all is well may manifest themselves by withdrawal from social interaction, depression, persistent headaches or stomach aches, unhappiness at school, behavioural problems or behaviour that is out of character.

- Children can blame themselves for a death. They need reassurance that they are not responsible.

- Children like to feel they are being helpful, comforting and supportive to others. Giving them genuinely helpful jobs makes them feel included and wanted.

- Adults can help prepare their children for the experience of death and grief by not avoiding it as a subject in the home, as though it were a secret for grown-ups. Often the death of a pet is a way in which to expose children to the reality of death and the sadness that follows.

- Adults may be fearful that children will be harmed or frightened by attending a funeral. However, children are quite resilient and generally prefer to stay within the family circle. More harm can be done by excluding them than allowing them to participate. It is a good policy to ask them what they would like to do. Explaining to them beforehand what is going to happen can be an enormous help.
- The difficulty adults have with talking about death with their children can be a reflection of their own inability to face issues of death.

Who and What Can Help?

Grieving takes time, and for each person it will be different, but there are many things you can do to ease your grief and to help you to move on.

Be Kind to Yourself

The experience of grief can drain us of energy and leave us feeling exhausted. As mentioned earlier, it can also disrupt our sleeping pattern. Having extra rest is not a weakness but a wise thing to do.

Our emotional and physical overload can also leave our immune system very low and make us vulnerable to illness. Eating well and taking some form of preventative supplement over this time will help.

Give yourself treats and do not be afraid to be self-indulgent if you feel able.

Professional Help

The journey through grief can feel like a hard uphill struggle. To help us get to the end, we may need help. There is no shame in asking for it. Most people appreciate short-term support: some of us will need longer-term help, especially if we get stuck on one of the stages of the journey.

Your GP will be well aware of how loss affects us and will be able to recommend medication and counselling support if required. There are some counselling organisations (see Useful

Addresses, pages 335–41) that specialise in helping those who are facing bereavement. We should not wait until we are falling apart before seeking support – indeed it is better not to wait until we are desperate.

When we find that our grief is so overwhelming or progress towards recovery does not seem to be happening, we may need to be referred to a psychiatrist or a psychotherapist.

A local priest or a person whom we consider a spiritual leader can also provide a listening ear and comfort that sustains our faith and gives us reassurance.

Most private counselling services will charge.

Helping Others to Grieve

In a society such as ours, where free expression of extreme emotion can cause discomfort, it is very hard to acknowledge the suffering of bereavement. We might allow those who have experienced a great loss to mourn for a short while, but generally we expect people to behave decorously in grief and to be brave and to take things well. This stiff upper lip phenomenon is not actually Victorian, as is sometimes thought, but was most evident during the First World War.

However, this is not always the best way to cope – it is much healthier for people to be free to grieve openly – and contemporary experts in counselling and psychotherapy cite Princess Diana's death in 1997 as the key that unlocked a door that had been firmly shut since the early 20th century, and the torrent of emotion that followed her passing heralded a new dawn in our emotional awareness. We must take forward and not forget the lessons we have learned. We must support families in the midst of their sorrow and take care of them, allowing them room for their pain.

We may be the person who has experienced the loss and be the recipient of the support of others or we may be the one giving the help. If we find ourselves as the giver, the following guidelines may help:

- seek out the mourner and listen without judgment to what they say
- avoid giving advice
- allow the mourner to talk, even to go repeatedly over the same ground
- do not advise them to stifle tears – assure them that it is all right to weep
- do not tell them to pull themselves together
- acknowledge their pain and loss
- do not assume you know how they are feeling: instead, ask them how they are feeling
- accept however they are feeling and go with it
- be careful not to share your own experience of loss too quickly and unless you sense it may be helpful
- encourage the mourner to participate in the practical arrangements for the funeral and to feel involved
- use the name of the deceased frequently and encourage talking about them; share memories
- use hugs and touch or hold hands – this can be affirming when a physical partner has died
- offer practical help but check out what would be most helpful
- avoid clearing up too quickly and wanting to dispense of the belongings of the deceased immediately
- reassure the mourner that decisions about the future do not have to be made now
- be natural and not over-anxious about finding the right words or phrases to use
- accept that grief is a long journey and that support will be needed for a long time, not just days or weeks

You will find many organisations, groups and books that may help in Useful Addresses and the Bibliography (see pages 335–41 and 342).

FUNERAL PLANNING CHECKLIST

Action	What you will need and why/decisions to be made	✔
Register the death	1. Take the Medical Certificate of Cause of Death, issued by the doctor.	
	2. Have enough money to cover the costs of Death Certificates. Order enough copies as you will need several (they are more expensive if ordered afterwards). Banks, building societies, etc. will all want an original copy so you need to think about the estate and decide how many is appropriate.	
	3. Have the following information:	
	• date and place of death	
	• name of deceased plus date and place of birth	
	• maiden name of a deceased female	
	• occupation of deceased (currently also name and occupation of a deceased female's husband)	
	• permanent address of deceased	
	• any pension or benefit details	
	• NHS number if possible	
Inform any other necessary authorities – bank, building societies, pension fund provider, Department of Social Security etc.	Take the original copy of the Death Certificate – proof will be needed.	

Action	What you will need and why/decisions to be made	✔
Make preliminary funeral plan	1. Burial or cremation? 2. Church, crematorium chapel or other venue? 3. Use or not of funeral director? 4. Finance: How will you pay? Have you access to funds? Might you require state assistance? 5. Check with bank – it will usually release money for a funeral from a frozen account providing there are funds available. 6. Suitable date and time for funeral. Be flexible if possible. 7. Crematoria usually allow a double booking (for a fee), which will give extra time and avoid rush.	
Contact funeral director	1. Take the green Certificate for Burial or Cremation issued by the registrar. The funeral director will need this before being able to proceed. 2. Agree a convenient date and time for you, the funeral director and the minister. 3. Select a funeral package. 4. Discuss finance and means of payment. Have a budget in mind and don't be swayed from this – stay with what you can afford. Ask for the price list. 5. Any questions – write them down. 6. Confirm that the funeral director will make arrangements with the local church or crematorium. 7. Choose the coffin and handles. 8. Decide on transport and staff requirements, including coffin bearers. 9. View and select from the funeral director's range of floral tributes, if wished.	
Contact family, friends, relatives, work colleagues and anyone else who might wish to come to the funeral	1. Inform them of the date, time and location for the funeral. 2. Send directions and/or a map, if necessary, including to the reception. 3. Let them know about flowers/donations to a charity. (Ask family and friends for help with ringing round. It can be time-consuming and distressing having to repeat the news.)	

Action	What you will need and why/decisions to be made	✔
Choose any hymns, music and readings	1. If you have already made choices, check with the minister that they are suitable. 2. If necessary, ask the minister or organist for ideas. See also Part 3 of this book.	
Plan service sheets	1. Professionally printed or self-published? 2. Find suitable photographs, poems and quotations to include. 3. Decoration – simple or fancy?	
The tribute/eulogy	Who will deliver it? Topics to think about: • childhood • family and locality • growing up • work and colleagues • clubs and societies • marriage or partnership/relationships • children • pets • what mattered to the deceased • how you felt about the deceased • how you will remember the deceased • anecdotes that characterise the deceased • any other things – idiosyncrasies, likes, dislikes etc.	
Flowers	• Funeral director to provide? • If the church/crematorium has a flower-arranging rota, enquire if some of the ladies might be prepared to see to the flowers for you. Let them know your preferences. Check costs. • Florists – what services do they provide? • Ask friends to do flowers. • Use flowers from your own garden and self-arrange. • Donations instead of flowers?	

Action	What you will need and why/decisions to be made	✔
Contact minister	1. Make sure he or she is happy with the choice of hymns and readings. 2. Have any other questions about the funeral ready.	
Transport	How many might need transport to the venue? Check with the funeral director for more information.	
Reception	1. Find out numbers likely to attend, if possible. 2. At home or in a room in a local pub or hotel? 3. If a hotel or pub, telephone to find out whether a suitable sized room is available and what kind of food they can lay on at relatively short notice, plus a price per head. 4. If at home, choose food that can be frozen if left over. Buy alcohol but make sure soft drinks and tea and coffee are also available. (Remember that some supermarkets offer sale or return on alcohol.) 5. If at home, will you need to hire or borrow glasses, cups and saucers, cutlery etc? (Some supermarkets and off licences also loan glasses.)	
Book of remembrance	A sort of visitor's book for the day. Ask that people note their addresses as well so you can drop them a brief note at a later date should you feel up to it.	
Camera and film	You might want to take a few photographs of the flowers etc.	

Action	What you will need and why/decisions to be made	✔
Clothes	1. What will you and the family wear? 2. Will you need to shop? You may have to factor in a trip so allow time for that.	
Thank you letters	• You might like to write to the hospital, funeral director, minister or anyone else who helped, either during a last illness or with the funeral itself. • It is usual to write to thank those who sent floral tributes.	

PART 3
READINGS AND
MUSICAL IDEAS

CHOOSING READINGS

There are certain times in life when we find it hard to find the right words to use. There is no time when this is truer than when someone we love or know dies. We may be so shocked or upset that words fail us altogether. Shakespeare wrote of a 'grief that does not speak'. Our deepest feelings are always difficult to put into words. That is why we often express those feelings with symbols such as flowers or pictures or with music. Poetry too will often communicate our feelings in a way that cannot be conveyed by other writing.

We should not be surprised that when death occurs our mind goes blank as we seek anxiously for an appropriate verse or reading that will put into words a little of how we feel. When we are planning for the funeral itself, we may also find ourselves at a loss for some reading that will connect with what we want to say about the one we have lost. It is not easy and we should not feel guilty or ashamed if no suitable readings or words immediately come to mind.

The Purpose of the Readings

The purpose of the collection of readings that follow is to provide you with some help. It is a selection of popular readings and others that are less familiar. Making a choice may take some time as you read through or something may strike you instantly as being just right. It is wise to give yourself time. Sometimes by reading a passage or poem several times, you will discover deeper layers of meaning.

What we all want to do is to choose the very best readings that we feel most accurately express the thoughts in our hearts and minds. No words, however many, are adequate to sum up the life and personality of a person. Words cannot encapsulate fully all that we understand by character and personality. We struggle and strain to convey what somebody meant to us. There is something about the mysterious uniqueness of each person that cannot be contained in words. Words rarely express the love we feel or the heartbreaking loss and huge gap that the death of a loved one leaves. We want, however, to say something and finding appropriate readings for the funeral is very important.

Choosing Your Readings

The readings are divided into three sections. There is a selection of prose readings, followed by a larger choice of readings that are poetry, verses or lines that express someone's thoughts about death and dying. Finally, there is a wide choice of readings from the Bible. People of other faiths or none can use their own resources but we hope they may also find something helpful in the other sections of this book.

Most of the readings can be used on the occasion of any death. Others relate specifically to parents, children, spouses, friends, pets or other relationships. When thinking about who will deliver the readings, it is wise to consult with others who have played a significant part in the life of the deceased. Often, a relation or friend will consider it an honour to be asked to do a reading. However, it is not unusual for people to feel too emotional to take on a reading. In this case, the leader or minister at the service will usually be willing to help.

As a rule, funeral services will allow for one or more readings, though much will depend on the length of the reading or readings you would like included and the time available for the whole of the service. It is important to consult the person who is conducting the service and inform them about your choices.

We Cannot 'Say It All'

At the funeral of a loved one, there is often so much that we would like to say both in our tributes or eulogies and in our choice of the readings. We may have to accept that we cannot 'say it all' and that many tributes and precious thoughts remain in the silence of our hearts. However, we hope that from the readings we have gathered here, you will find one or more pieces that express something of your thoughts and feelings for the person whose funeral you are planning or attending.

PROSE READINGS

And God Created Mothers

When the good Lord was creating mothers, he was into his sixth day of overtime when an angel appeared and said, 'You're doing a lot of fiddling around on this one.'

And the Lord said, 'Have you read the specification on this order? She has to be completely washable, but no plastic ... have one hundred and eighty movable parts – all replaceable ... run on black coffee and leftovers ... have a lap that disappears when she stands up ... a kiss that can cure anything from a broken leg to a disappointed love affair ... and six pairs of hands.'

The angel shook her head slowly and said, 'Six pairs of hands? No way.'

'It's not the hands that are causing me problems,' said the Lord. 'It's the three pairs of eyes that mothers have to have.'

'That's on the standard model?' asked the angel.

The Lord nodded. 'One pair that sees through doors when she asks, "What are you children doing in there?" when she already knows. Another in the back of her head that sees what she shouldn't but what she has to know. And, of course, the ones in front that can look at a child when he gets himself into trouble and say "I understand and I love you" without so much as uttering a word.'

'Lord,' said the angel, touching him gently, 'go to bed. Tomorrow is another day.'

'I can't. I'm so close now. Already I have one who heals herself when she is sick, can feed a family of six on one pound of mince, and can get a nine-year old to have a bath,' said the Lord. The angel circled the model very slowly.

'It's too soft,' she sighed.

'But tough,' said the Lord, excitedly. 'You cannot imagine what this mother can do and endure.'

'Can it think?'

'Not only think but it can reason and compromise,' said the Creator.

Finally the angel bent over and ran her finger across the cheek. 'There's a leak,' she said.

'It's not a leak,' replied the Lord. 'It's a tear.'

'What's it for?'

'It's for joy, sadness, disappointment, pain, loneliness and pride.'

'You're a genius!' said the angel.

The Lord looked sombre – 'I didn't put it there.'

ANONYMOUS

The Bonds of Love

Nothing can make up for the absence of someone whom we love, and it would be wrong to try to find a substitute; we must simply hold out and see it through. That sounds very hard at first, but at the same time it is a great consolation, for the gap, as long as it remains unfilled, preserves the bonds between us. It is nonsense to say that God fills the gap; God doesn't fill it, but on the contrary, keeps it empty and so helps us to keep alive our former communion with each other, even at the cost of pain.

DIETRICH BONHOEFFER (1906–1945)

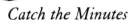

Catch the Minutes

Don't cry, Columbine. I shall go away with a smile on my lips. I want to die as people want to sleep, when it is late and they are tired and need rest.

I have sung all my songs, I have revelled all my merriment, I have laughed all my laughter.

My health and my strength have been joyfully spent with my money. I was never mean and so was always merry and sorrowless.

Do not cry, Columbine, rather be glad that I am dying not like others, but full of delight, content with fate and my conduct. Or would you rather see me grappling with life with greedy eyes and a prayer on my lips?

No, Harlequin is not like that. He has fulfilled his mission in life and dies calmly. And really, didn't I give my kisses to those who wanted them? Didn't I lavish my soul for the good of others? How many wives of ugly husbands have I consoled? How many hats did I make for people who thought they were sages? How many did I give an example? Now I have outlived my life and only the husk is left for death. 'Catch the minutes', that's my motto, and I've not been idle to catch them. I've caught so many that I want no more.

Now, perhaps another kiss, a little draught of wine, a burst of merry laughter and it will be the end.

NICHOLAS EVREINOFF (1879–1953)

Death Can Enrich Us

Death can cast us down for more than the necessary period of mourning. It can blight our days, so that we exist forever in that chill, unexpected land. It can whisper to us that life is ultimately meaningless. If what awaits us at the end is our own obliteration, and the same grief we now feel is transferred like a disease to those who love us, what is the point of going on, of ambition, of rearing children who too will one day fail and fall? It can hang like an albatross about our necks; or enclose our hearts in ice; or change us so deeply that even our closest friends turn away. At its worst, death has taken one life; and is offered another.

And yet it can enrich us. We can live for those who have gone. We can pack into our lives that extra time the dead have given us. For they have given time: the expanded moment that comes when we realise that, for us, the blood still moves; the world is still there to be explored and made over; that, for now this minute, this hour, this day, we are free of pain and hunger; that, though we still mourn in the deepest part of our being, death has liberated us, has made us see the transitory nature of everything; and life, being transitory, is thus infinitely more precious; commanding more attention than ever we gave it when we went on our way, still unthinking children, before death opened our minds, sharpened our eyes; and set us free.

CHRISTOPHER LEACH (b. 1925)
From *Letter to a Younger Son*

Death Cannot Kill What Never Dies

They that love beyond the world cannot be separated by it.
Death cannot kill what never dies. Nor can spirits ever be
divided that love and live in the same divine principle: the root
and record of their friendship.

Death is but a crossing the world as friends do seas; they
live in one another still. For they must needs be present that
love and live in that which is omnipresent. In this divine glass
they see face to face; and their converse is free as well as pure.
This is the comfort of friends, that though they may be said to
die, yet their friendship and society are, in the best sense, ever
present, because immortal.

WILLIAM PENN (1644–1718)
From *Fruits of Solitude – Part II – Union of Friends*

Death is Part of the Future

Death is part of the future for everyone. It is the last post of
this life and the reveille of the next. Everywhere men fear
death – it is the end of our present life, it is parting from loved
ones, it is setting out into the unknown. We overcome death by
accepting it as the will of a loving God; by finding him in it.
Death, like birth, is only a transformation, another birth.
When I die I shall change my state, that is all. And in faith in
God, it is as easy and natural as going to sleep here and waking
up there.

GEORGE APPLETON (1902–1993)
From *Journey for a Soul*

Death, Where is Thy Sting?

Then said he, 'I am going to my Father's and, though with great difficulty I am got hither, yet now I do not repent me of all the trouble I have been at, to arrive where I am. My sword I give to him that shall succeed me in my pilgrimage, and my courage and skill to him that can get it. My marks and scars I carry with me, to be a witness for me, that I have fought His battles, who now will be my rewarder.'

When the day that he must go hence was come, many accompanied him to the riverside, into which as he went he said 'Death, where is thy sting?'. And as he went down deeper, he said, 'Grave, where is thy victory?'. So, he passed over, and all the trumpets sounded for him on the other side.

JOHN BUNYAN (1628–1688)
From *The Pilgrim's Progress*

Divine Love Cannot Change

Loving with human love, one may pass from love to hatred; but divine love cannot change. Nothing, not even death, can shatter it. It is the very nature of the soul... Love is life. All, all that I understand, I understand only because I love. All is, all exists only because I love. All is bound up in love alone. Love is God, and dying means for me a particle of love, to go back to the universal and eternal source of love.

LEO TOLSTOY (1828–1910)
From *War and Peace*

Footprints in the Sand

One night a man had a dream.

He dreamed he was walking along the beach with the Lord.

Across the sky flashed scenes from his life.

For each scene he noticed two sets of footprints in the sand: one belonging to him and the other to the Lord.

When the last scene of his life flashed before him, he looked back at the footprints in the sand.

He noticed that many times along the path of his life there was only one set of footprints.

He also noticed that it happened at the very lowest and saddest times of his life.

This really bothered him and he questioned the Lord about it.

'Lord, you said that once I decided to follow you, you'd walk with me all the way. But I have noticed that during the most troublesome times in my life there is only one set of footprints. I don't understand why when I needed you most you would leave me.'

The Lord replied, 'My son, precious child, I love you and I would never leave you! During your times of trial and suffering, when you see only one set of footprints, it was then that I carried you.'

MARY STEVENSON (1922–1999)

A Gateway to a Better Place

Death is a formidable foe until we learn to make it a friend.
Death is to be feared if we do not learn to welcome it. Death is
the ultimate absurdity if we do not see it as fulfilment. Death
haunts us when viewed as a journey into nothingness rather
than a pilgrimage to a place where true happiness is to be
found.

The human mind cannot understand death. We face it with
fear and uncertainty, revulsion even; or we turn away from the
thought for it is too hard to bear.

But faith gives answers when reason fails. The strong
instinct to live points to immortality. Faith admits us into
death's secrets. Death is not the end of the road, but a gateway
to a better place. It is in this place that our noblest aspirations
will be realised.

It is here that we will understand how our experiences of
goodness, love, beauty and joy are realities which exist perfectly
in God. It is in heaven that we shall rest in him and our hearts
will be restless until they rest in God.

CARDINAL GEORGE BASIL HUME (1923–1999)
From *The Mystery of the Cross*

Go On with What You Are Doing

Go on with what you are doing. Work faithfully in my
vineyard, and I shall be your reward. Write, read and sing;
lament your sins, keep silence, pray; bravely endure all that you
find hard to bear – eternal life is worth all these and greater
struggles too. Peace will come to you on a day which is already
known to the Lord, and for them there will be no day or night
such as you know on this earth, but perpetual light, splendour
without end, peace that cannot be broken, calm that holds no
fear. You will not then say, 'Who is to set me free from a nature
thus doomed to death?' nor will you cry, 'Unhappy I, that live
in exile'; for death shall be engulfed, and salvation be complete.
Then there will be no fear, but blessed joy and sweet
companionship, full of pure delight.

THOMAS À KEMPIS (1379–1471)
From *The Imitation of Christ*

A Helping Hand

I have no fear of death – but I shall welcome a helping hand to
see me through.
For it is said that just as everyone has a guardian angel, so to
each one comes somebody to help us over the stile.
Once I am over, I know a door will open on a new loveliness
and freshness of colour, form and light which is far more
beautiful than anything I have ever seen or imagined.

OLIVER HALL
From *The Wind in the Oak*

I Am Standing Upon that Foreshore

I am standing upon that foreshore. A ship at my side spreads her white sails in the morning breeze and starts for the blue ocean. She is an object of beauty and strength and I stand and watch her until at length she hangs like a speck of white cloud just where the sea and sky come down to mingle with each other. Then someone at my side says:

'There! She is gone!'

'Gone where?'

'Gone from my sight, that's all.'

She is just as large in mast and spar and hull as ever she was when she left my side; just as able to bear her load of living freight to the place of her destination. Her diminished size is in me, not in her. And just at that moment when someone at my side says, 'There! She is gone!' there are other eyes watching her coming and other voices ready to take up the glad shout:

'Here she comes!'

And that is dying.

VICTOR HUGO (1802–1885)
From *Toilers of the Sea*

I See Myself Now at the End of My Journey

I see myself now at the end of my journey, my toilsome days are ended. I am going now to see that head that was crowned with thorns, and that face that was spit upon for me.

I have formerly lived by hearsay and faith but now I go where I shall live by sight, and shall be with him in whose company I delight myself.

I have loved to hear my Lord spoken of; and wherever I have seen the print of his shoe in the earth, there I have coveted to set my foot to.

His name to me has been as a civet-box; yea, sweeter than all perfume. His voice to me has been most sweet; and his countenance I have more desired than they that have most desired the light of the sun. His word I did use to gather for my food, and for antidotes against my faintings. 'He has held me, and hath kept me from mine iniquities; yea, my steps hath he strengthened in his way.'

Glorious it was to see how the open region was filled with horses and chariots, with trumpeters and pipers, with singers and players on stringed instruments, to welcome the pilgrims as they went up and followed one another in at the beautiful gate of the city.

JOHN BUNYAN (1628–1688)
From *The Pilgrim's Progress* (read at the Queen Mother's funeral)

It Seems Such a Waste

It seems such waste, such stupid senseless waste. His great thoughts, his fine body that loved life, all the friendship, the aspiration, the love … all thrown away, gone, wasted for ever.

Who says that it is wasted? It is his body that has served its turn and is cast away. The great thoughts, the friendship, the aspiration, the love; can we say that these die? Nay, rather, these shall not die. These shall live in the Courts of the Lord, forever.

EDITH NESBIT (1858–1924)

Look to This Day!

Look to this day! For it is life, the very life of life. In its brief course lie all the varieties and realities of your existence: the bliss of growth, the glory of action, the splendour of beauty. For yesterday is already a dream, and tomorrow is only a vision, but today, well-lived, makes every yesterday a dream of happiness, and every tomorrow a vision of hope.

Look well, therefore, to this day! Such is the salutation of the dawn.

From the SANSKRIT

Lord, We Turn to You

Lord, we turn to You in our grief and our bewilderment, for a mystery surrounds the birth and death of man. Your will summons us into this world and then calls us to depart, but Your plan is so vast and Your purposes so deep that our understanding fails, and our reason cannot follow. Yet You have taught us that time and space are not the measure of all things. Beyond them is the life of eternity. We do not die into the grave but into the love of God.

It has been Your will to receive the soul of her/him, to bring her/him to life everlasting, and she/he is beyond the tragedies of this world. We find our comfort in Your teaching. Beyond the grave we shall meet together in the life that has no end.

From the *Jewish Funeral Service Prayer Book*

Man is Spiritual Here and Now

Believing as I do that man is spiritual here and now wherever he may seem to be, I have no doubts that [name] is simply continuing in the continuity of life; and, that is, in the spiritual realm where she has always essentially been. We think we love someone for their looks; their walk maybe; tone of voice, touch – but when you analyse it is really for their qualities – their warmth, their humour, their intelligence, kindness, etcetera. These things are spiritual qualities and are recognisable only by the spiritual in us. This, to me, is proof of spirituality. We may think it's the shape of a person's nose or the way the eyes light up or whatever it is, but in fact it is the impression these things have on us and this is not physical or material, is it? So – although the sense of loss is brutal and a shock – when you can look at it and think of it and feel the very real gratitude you have for having known and loved someone, then I think a sense of *real* reality takes over and one comes to the reasonable conclusion that spirituality is a reality; a continuing reality of all-good.

I believe the way to peace is not to mourn, but to free her in your mind and heart and realise she is always whole, always real because she is spiritual – and so are you.

We don't become spiritual when we die. We have always been spiritual and that, as I see it, is what life is for – to discover and rejoice in this. It leads into harmonious living now. It reveals what is actually real and durable.

JOYCE GRENFELL (1910–1979)
From *Joyce: by Herself and Her Friends*

The Merriment of Old Age

It is commonly said that hope goes with youth, and lends to
youth its wings of a butterfly: but I fancy that hope is the last
gift given to man and the only gift not given to youth. Youth is
pre-eminently the period in which a man can be lyric, fanatical,
poetic; but youth is a period in which a man can be hopeless.
The end of every episode is the End of the World. But the
power of hoping through everything, the knowledge that the
soul survives its adventures, this great inspiration comes to the
middle-aged; God has kept this good wine until now. It is from
the backs of the elderly gentlemen that the wings of the
butterfly should burst. There is nothing that so much mystifies
the young as the constant frivolity of the old. They have
discovered their indestructibility. They are in their second and
clearer childhood, and there is a meaning in the merriment of
their eyes. They have seen the end of the End of the World.

G. K. CHESTERTON (1874–1936)

A New Belonging

The deaths of those whom we love and who love us, open up the possibility of a new, more radical communion, a new intimacy, a new belonging to each other. If love is, indeed, stronger than death, then death has the potential to deepen and strengthen the bonds of love.

The death of the beloved bears fruit in many lives. You and I have to trust that our short little lives can bear fruit far beyond the boundaries of our chronologies. But we have to choose this and trust deeply that we have a spirit to send that will bring joy, peace and life to those who will remember us.

HENRI NOUWEN (1932–1996)
From *Life of the Beloved*

No Man is an Island

All mankind is of one Author, and is one volume; when one man dies, one chapter is not torn out of the book, but translated into a better language; and every chapter must be so translated; God employs several translators; some pieces are translated by age, some by sickness, some by war, some by justice; but God's hand is in every translation; and his hand shall bind up all our scattered leaves again, for that Library where every book shall lie open to one another.

No man is an island, entire of itself; every man is a piece of the continent, a part of the main; if a clod be washed away by the sea, Europe is the less, as well as if a promontory were, as well as if a manor of thine friends or of thine own were; any man's death diminishes me, because I am involved in Mankind; and therefore never send to know for whom the bell tolls; it tolls for thee.

JOHN DONNE (1572–1631)

Of Children

And a woman who held a babe against her bosom said, 'Speak
to us of Children.'

And He said: 'Your children are not your children,

They are the sons and daughters of Life's longing for itself.

They come through you but not from you,

And though they are with you,

Yet they belong not to you.

You may give them your love but not your thoughts,

For they have their own thoughts.

You may house their bodies but not their souls,

For their souls dwell in the house of tomorrow,

Which you cannot visit, not even in your dreams.

You may strive to be like them, but seek not to make them like
you.

For life goes not backward nor tarries with yesterday.

You are the bows from which your children as living arrows
are sent forth.

The Archer sees the mark upon the path of the infinite, and
He bends you with all His might,

That His arrow may go swift and far.

Let your bending in the Archer's hand be for gladness;

For even as He loves the arrow that flies,

So He loves also the bow that is stable.'

KAHLIL GIBRAN (1883–1931)
From *The Prophet*

Of Death

Then Aimitra spoke, saying, 'We would ask now of Death.'
  And He said:
'You would know the secret of death. But how shall you find it
  unless you seek it in the heart of life?

The owl whose night-bound eyes are blind unto the day cannot
  unveil the mystery of light.

If you would indeed behold the spirit of death, open your heart
  wide unto the body of life.

For life and death are one, even as the river and the sea are one.

In the depth of your hopes and desires lies your silent
  knowledge of the beyond;

And like seeds dreaming beneath the snow your heart dreams
  of spring.

Trust the dreams, for in them is hidden the gate to eternity.

Your fear of death is but the trembling of the shepherd when
  he stands before the king whose hand is laid upon him in
  honour.

Is the shepherd not joyful beneath his trembling, that he shall
  wear the mark of the king?

Yet is he not more mindful of his trembling?

For what is it to die but stand naked in the wind and to melt in
  the sun?

And what is it to cease breathing but to free the breath from its
  restless tides, that it may rise and expand and seek God
  unencumbered?

Only when you drink from the river of silence shall you indeed
  sing. And when you have reached the mountain top, then
  you shall begin to climb.

And when the earth shall claim your limbs, then you shall
  truly dance.'

KAHLIL GIBRAN (1883–1931)
From *The Prophet*

Of Friendship

And a youth said, 'Speak to us of Friendship.'

And He answered, saying:

'Your friend is your needs answered.

He is your field which you sow with love and reap
    with thanksgiving.

And he is your board and your fireside.

For you come to him with your hunger, and you seek
    him for peace.

When your friend speaks his mind you fear not the
    'nay' in your mind, nor do you withhold the
    'ay'.

And when he is silent your heart ceases not to listen
    to his heart;

For without words, in friendship, all thoughts, all
    desires, all expectations are born and shared,
    with joy that is unacclaimed.

When you part from your friend, you grieve not;

For that which you love most in him may be clearer
    in his absence, as the mountain to the climber
    is clearer from the plain.

And let there be no purpose in friendship save the
    deepening of the spirit.

KAHLIL GIBRAN (1883–1931)
From *The Prophet*

The Old Pattern and the New

We are one people, one community, and the death of one is the
concern of all. In the face of death man can achieve grandeur,
but if he turns his back on death he remains a child, clinging to
a land of make-believe. For death is not the ending of the
pattern of life's unwinding, but a necessary interruption.
Through the painful work of grieving we rediscover the past
and weave it afresh into a new reality.

Our aim cannot be to cancel out the past, to try to forget,
but to ensure that the strength and meaning which gave beauty
to the old pattern is remembered and reinterpreted in the
pattern now emerging. Every man must die but the world is
permanently changed by each man's existence. At the point of
death we meet the forces of social evolution. We may back
away in fear, refuse the chance to change, drown our pain in
drugs or alcohol or meaningless activity, or we may accept the
pains of grief and begin the long struggle to rediscover
meaning in a life whose meanings can no longer be taken for
granted. There is no easy way through the long valley but we
have faith in the ability of each one to find his own way, given
time and the encouragement of the rest of us.

COLIN MURRAY PARKES – President of Cruse Bereavement Care

Our Life Must Be a Continuation of Theirs

With every person who dies, part of us is already in eternity.
We must, if we love this person, live up to the great encounter
of a living soul with a living God. We must let go of everything
that was small, that was separation, alienation and
estrangement, and reach out to that serenity and greatness,
newness and abundance of life into which the departed person
has entered. We should not speak of our love in the past tense.
Love is a thing that does not fade in a faithful heart. It does not
go into the past unless we betray our love. We must keep our
love alive in a new situation, but as actively and creatively, and
more so, more often, than when the person was with us. Our
love cannot be dead because a person has died. If that is true,
our life must be a continuation of theirs, with all its
significance. We must reflect on all that was beauty, and
nobility, in that person, and make sure those around us, and
our surroundings, do not lose anything through the death. This
applies to all families and friends as well as the immediate
bereaved, so that the seed that has fallen into corruption may
give a hundredfold harvest in the hearts and lives of others.

METROPOLITAN ANTHONY OF SOUROZH (1914–2003)
From *Modern Man Facing Death*

The Significant Hours of Our Life

I always think that we all live, spiritually, by what others have given us in the significant hours of our life. These significant hours do not announce themselves as coming, but arrive unexpectedly. Nor do they make a great show of themselves; they pass almost unperceived. Often, indeed, their significance comes home to us first as we look back, just as the beauty of a piece of music or a landscape often strikes us first in our recollection of it. Much that has become our own in gentleness, modesty, kindness, willingness to forgive, in veracity, loyalty, resignation under suffering, we owe to people in whom we have seen and experienced these virtues at work, sometimes in a great matter, sometimes in a small. A thought which had become an act sprang into us like a spark, and lit a new flame within us...

If we had before us those who have thus been a blessing to us, and could tell them how it came about, they would be amazed to learn what passed over from their life into ours.

ALBERT SCHWEITZER (1875–1965)

Speak to Us of Joy and Sorrow

Then a woman said, 'Speak to us of Joy and Sorrow.'

And He answered:

'Your joy is your sorrow unmasked.

And the selfsame well from which your laughter rises was
oftentimes filled with your tears.

And how else can it be?

The deeper that sorrow carves into your being, the more joy
you can contain.

Is not the cup that holds your wine the very cup that was
burned in the potter's oven?

And is not the lute that soothes your spirit the very wood that
was hollowed by knives?

When you are joyous, look deep into your heart and you shall
find it is only that which has given you sorrow that is
giving you joy.'

KAHLIL GIBRAN (1883–1931)

From *The Prophet*

There is No Effort without Error

It is not the critic who counts, nor the man who points out how the strong man stumbles, or where the doer of deeds could have done them better. The credit belongs to the man who is actually in the arena, whose face is marred by dust and sweat and blood, who strives valiantly; who errs and comes short again and again: because there is no effort without error and shortcomings: but who does actually strive to do the deed: who knows the great enthusiasm, the great devotion, who spends himself in a worthy cause, who at the best knows in the end the triumph of high achievement and who at the worst, if he fails, at least he fails while daring greatly. So that his place shall never be with those cold and timid souls who know neither victory nor defeat.

THEODORE ROOSEVELT (1858–1919)

We Seem to Give Them Back to You

We seem to give them back to you, O God, who gave them to us. As you did not lose them in giving, so do we not lose them by their return. Not as the world gives, give you, O lover of souls.

What you give, you take not away, for what is yours is ours also if we belong to you. And life is eternal and love is immortal, and death is only an horizon. An horizon is nothing, save the limit of our sight.

Lift us up, strong Son of God, that we may see further; cleanse our eyes that we may see more clearly; draw us closer to you that we may know ourselves to be nearer to our loved ones who are with you. And while you prepare a place for us, prepare us also for that happy place, that where you are we may be also for ever more.

WILLIAM PENN (1644–1718)

What We Begin Here, We Shall Finish Hereafter

If death should end all, then human life here would become
meaningless. If we were born to play a little, learn a little, grow
up, sin, work, love, hope, and soon lie still in death, then those
valiant ones who have striven for character and service above
selfish ease and the comfort of life, were just fools. What is the
use of discipline and self-giving here, if there is no after-life
where all these lovely developed powers can be used. Life's
noblest efforts seem paralysed. When God gave us these
splendid yearnings and hopes, we believe He was not just
blowing bubbles – pretty to look upon, but of no permanence.
To feel less would be inconsistent with what we know of God
the Father, through Christ now risen. 'To no companion of
earth's short journey' we believe, 'need we give an everlasting
farewell. What we begin here, we shall finish hereafter, if
indeed it be worth the finishing.'

RITA F. SNOWDEN (1907–1999)
From *When Sorrow Comes*

When He Calls Us, We May Go Unfrightened

May He give us all the courage that we need to go the way He
shepherds us. That, when He calls us, we may go
unfrightened. If He bids us come to Him across the waters,
that unfrightened we may go. And if He bids us climb the hill,
may we not notice that it is a hill, mindful only of the
happiness of His company. He made us for Himself, that we
should travel with Him and see Him at last in His unveiled
beauty in the abiding city where he is light and happiness and
endless home.

BEDE JARRETT (1881–1934)

You Were Very Special

In all the world there was nobody, nobody like you. Since the beginning of time there had never been another person like you. Nobody had your smile, your eyes, your hands, your hair. Nobody owned your handwriting, your voice. You were special.

Nobody could paint your brush stokes. Nobody had your taste for food or music or dance or art. Nobody in the universe saw things as you did. In all time there had never been anyone who laughed in exactly your way, and what made you laugh or cry or think could have a totally different response in another. So you were special.

You were different from any other person who had ever lived in the history of the universe. You were the only one in the whole creation who had your particular set of abilities. There was always someone who was better at one thing or another. Every person was your superior in at least one way. But nobody in the universe ever had the combination of your talents, your feelings: like a roomful of musical instruments, some might excel in one way or another but nobody could match your symphony. Through all eternity no one would ever walk, talk, think or do exactly like you. You were special.

You were rare and in all rarity there is enormous value and because of your great value the need for you to imitate anyone else was absolutely wrong. You were special and it was no accident that you were. God made you for a special purpose. He had a job for you to do that nobody else could do as well as you could. Out of billions of applicants only one was qualified. Only one had the unique and right combination of what it took and that one was you.

You were very special.

Adapted by Alison Gibbs from *You are Very Special* by author unknown

POETRY READINGS

Abou Ben Adhem

Abou Ben Adhem (may his tribe increase!)
Awoke one night from a deep dream of peace,
And saw, within the moonlight in his room,
Making it rich, and like a lily in bloom,
And angel writing in a book of gold.
Exceeding peace had made Ben Adhem bold,
And to the presence in the room he said,
    'What writest thou?' – The vision raised its head,
And with a look made of all sweet accord,
Answered, 'The names of those who love the Lord.'
'And is mine one?' said Abou. 'Nay, not so,'
Replied the angel. Abou spoke more low,
But cheerily still; and said, 'I pray thee, then,
    Write me as one that loves his fellow men.'
The angel wrote, and vanished. The next night
It came again with a great wakening light,
And showed the names whom love of God had blest,
And lo! Ben Adhem's name led all the rest.

JAMES LEIGH HUNT (1784–1895)

Adieu and Au Revoir

As you love me, let there be
No mourning when I go –
No tearful eyes, no hopeless sighs,
No woe, nor even sadness.
Indeed, I would not have you sad,
For I myself shall be full glad
With the high triumphant gladness
Of a soul made free
Of God's sweet liberty.
No windows darkened, for my own
Will be flung wide, as ne'er before,
To catch the radiant in-pour
Of Love that shall in full atone
For all the ills that I have done.
No voices hushed; my own, full-flushed
With an immortal hope, will rise
In ecstasies of new-born bliss
And joyful melodies.
Rather, of your sweet courtesy
Rejoice with me
At my soul's loosing from captivity.
Wish me 'bon voyage' as you do a friend
Whose joyous visit finds its happy end
And bid me both 'adieu' and 'au revoir'
Since, though I come no more,
I shall be waiting there to greet you
At His door.
[And, as the feet of the bearers tread
The ways I trod,
Think not of me as dead, but rather –
Happy, thrice happy, he whose course is sped
He has gone home – to God
His Father.]

ATTRIB. JOHN OXENHAM (1852–1941)

After Glow

I'd like the memory of me
    to be a happy one.
I'd like to leave an after glow
    of smiles when life is done.
I'd like to leave an echo
    whispering softly down the ways,
Of happy times and laughing times
    and bright and sunny days.
I'd like the tears of those who grieve,
    to dry before the sun
Of happy memories
    That I leave when life is done.

ANON

All the World's a Stage

What is our life? A play of passion.

And what our mirth but music of division?

Our mothers' wombs the tiring houses be

Where we are dressed for this short comedy.

Heaven the judicious sharp spectator is

Who sits and marks what here we do amiss.

The graves that hide us from the searching sun

Are like drawn curtains when the play is done.

Thus playing post we to our latest rest,

And then we die in earnest, not in jest.

SIR WALTER RALEIGH (1552–1618)

And Death Shall Have No Dominion

And death shall have no dominion.
Dead men naked they shall be one
With the man in the wind and the west moon;
When their bones are picked clean and the clean bones gone,
They shall have stars at elbow and foot;
Though they go mad they shall be sane,
Though they sink through the sea they shall rise again;
Though lovers be lost love shall not;
And death shall have no dominion.
And death shall have no dominion.

Under the windings of the sea
They lying long shall not die windily;
Twisting on racks when sinews give way,
Strapped to a wheel, yet they shall not break;
Faith in their hands shall snap in two,
And the unicorn evils run them through;
Split all ends up they shan't crack;
And death shall have no dominion.
And death shall have no dominion.

No more may gulls cry at their ears
Or waves break loud on the seashores;
Where blew a flower may a flower no more
Lift its head to the blows of the rain;
Though they be mad and dead as nails,
Heads of the characters hammer through daisies;
Break in the sun till the sun breaks down,
And death shall have no dominion.

DYLAN THOMAS (1914–1953)

Beyond

Beyond the night the grey dawn waits to steal across the sky –
Beyond the dawn – the day – and so the hours go rolling by –
With hands outstretched we seek a heaven hidden from our
      sight –
Beyond our pain – we know there must be peace and pure
      delight …
The thrill of Life's sweet mystery is in this reaching out –
Towards a Something real and good beyond our human
      doubt …
The questing mind takes wing – a soul aroused can know no
      rest –
And Death itself can never dim the ardour of the quest –
There's always a Beyond – we go on striving ceaselessly –
Towards a God – the consciousness of perfect harmony.

PATIENCE STRONG (1907–1990)

The Beyond

It seemeth such a little way to me
Across to that strange country – the Beyond;
And yet, not strange, for it has grown to be
The home of those whom I am so fond,
They make it seem familiar and most dear,
As journeying friends bring distant regions near.

So close it lies, that when my sight is clear
I think I almost see the gleaming strand.
I know I feel those who have gone from here
Come near enough sometimes, to touch my hand
I often think, but for our veiled eyes,
We should find heaven right round about us lies.

I cannot make it seem a day to dread,
When from this dear earth I shall journey out
To that still dear country of the dead,
And join the lost ones, so long dreamed about.
I love this world, yet shall I love to go
And meet the friends who wait for me, I know.

I never stand above a bier and see
The seal of death set on some well-loved face
But that I think 'One more to welcome me,
When I shall cross the intervening space
Between this land and that one "over there";
One more to make the strange Beyond seem fair.'

And so for me there is no sting to death,
And so the grave has lost its victory.
It is but crossing – with bated breath,
And white, set face – a little strip of sea,
To find the loved ones waiting on the shore,
More beautiful, more precious than before.

ELLA WHEELER WILCOX (1850–1919)

A Child Loaned

'I'll lend you for a little time a child of Mine,' he said,

'For you to love the while she lives, and mourn for
     when she's dead.

She may be six or seven weeks, or thirteen years, or three,

But will you, till I call her back, take care of her for Me?

She'll bring her charm to gladden you, and should her
     stay be brief,

You'll have her lovely memories as solace for your grief.

I cannot promise she will stay, since all from Earth return,

But there are lessons taught down there I want this child
     to learn.

I looked the wide world over in my search for teachers true,

And from the throngs who crowd life's lanes I have
     selected you.

Now will you give her all your love, nor think the
     labour's vain,

Nor hate me when I come to call and take her back again?'

I fancied that I heard them say, 'Dear Lord, Thy will be done,

For all the joys Thy child shall bring the risk of grief we'll run.

We'll shelter her with tenderness, we'll love her
     while we may

And for the happiness we've known, forever grateful stay.

But, should the angels call for her much sooner than
     we planned

We'll brave the bitter grief that comes and try to understand.'

ANON

The Commemoration

In the rising of the sun and in its going down
    We remember them
In the blowing of the wind and in the chill of winter
    We remember them
In the blueness of the sky and in the warmth of summer
    We remember them
In the rustling of leaves and in the beauty of autumn
    We remember them
In the beginning of the year and when it ends
    We remember them
When we are lost and sick at heart
    We remember them
When we have joys we long to share
    We remember them
So long as we live, they too shall live, for they are part of us
    And we remember them

ANON

Crossing the Bar

Sunset and evening star,
And one clear call for me!
And may there be no moaning at the bar,
When I put out to sea,

But such a tide as moving seems asleep
Too full for sound and foam,
When that which drew from out the boundless deepn
Turns again home.

Twilight and evening bell,
And after that the dark!
And may there be no sadness of farewell
When I embark;

For though from out our bourne of time and place
The flood may bear me far,
I hope to see my Pilot face to face
When I have crossed the bar.

ALFRED, LORD TENNYSON (1809–1892)

The Dash Between the Years

I read of a man who stood to speak
At the funeral of his friend
He referred to the dates on his tombstone
From the beginning to the end.
He noted that first came his date of birth
And he spoke the following date with tears.
But he said what mattered most of all
Was the dash between those years.
For that dash represents all the time
That he spent alive on earth
And now only those who loved him
Know what that little line is worth.
For it matters not how much we own,
The cars, the house, the cash,
What matters is how we live and love
And how we spent our dash.
So think about this long and hard
Are there things you'd like to change?
For you never know how much time is left
That can still be rearranged.
If we could just slow down enough
To consider what's true and real
And always try to understand
The way other people feel,
And be less quick to anger,
And show appreciation more,
And love the people in our lives
Like we've never loved before.
If we treat each other with respect
And more often wear a smile
Remembering that this special dash
Might only last a little while.
So, when your eulogy is being read
With your life's actions to rehash
Would you be proud of the things they say
About how you spent your dash?

Anon

The Day You Left

With tears we saw you suffer,
As we watched you fade away,
Our hearts were almost broken,
As you fought so hard to stay.
We knew you had to leave us,
But you did not go alone,
For part of us went with you
The day you left your home.

ANON

The Dead

These hearts were woven of human joys and cares,
Washed marvellously with sorrow, swift to mirth.
The years had given them kindness. Dawn was theirs,
And sunset, and the colours of the earth.
These had seen movement, and heard music; known
Slumber and waking; loved; gone proudly friended;
Felt the quick stir of wonder; sat alone;
Touched furs and flowers and cheeks. All this is ended

There are waters blown by changing winds to laughter
And lit by the rich skies, all day. And after,
Frost, with a gesture, stays the waves that dance
And wandering loveliness. He leaves a white
Unbroken glory, a gathered radiance,
A width, a shining peace, under the night.

RUPERT BROOKE (1887–1915)

Death

Death, be not proud, though some have called thee
Mighty and dreadful, for thou art not so:
For those whom thou think'st thou dost overthrow
Die not, poor Death; nor yet canst thou kill me.
From rest and sleep, which but thy picture be,
Much pleasure, then from thee much more must flow;
And soonest our best men with thee do go –
Rest of their bones and soul's delivery!
Thou'rt slave to fate, chance, kings, and desperate men,
And dost with poison, war, and sickness dwell;
And poppy or charms can make us sleep as well
And better than thy stroke. Why swell'st thou then?
　　One short sleep is past, we wake eternally,
　　And death shall be no more: Death, thou shalt die!

JOHN DONNE (1572–1631)

Death Is Nothing At All

Death is nothing at all …
I have only slipped away into the next room.
I am I, and you are you.
Whatever we were to each other, that we are still.
Call me by my old familiar name.
Speak to me in the easy way which you always used.
Put no differences into your tone.
Wear no forced air of solemnity or sorrow.
Laugh as we always laughed at the little jokes we enjoyed
   together.
Play, smile, think of me, pray for me.
Let my name be ever the household name that it always was.
Let it be spoken without effort, without the ghost of a
   shadow on it.
Life means all that it ever meant. It is the same as it always was.
There is absolutely unbroken continuity.
What is this death but a negligible accident?
Why should I be out of mind because I am out of sight?
I am waiting for you for an interval somewhere very near …
Just around the corner.
All is well.

HENRY SCOTT HOLLAND (1847–1918)

Departed Comrade!

Departed comrade! Thou, redeemed from pain
Shall sleep the sleep that kings desire in vain:
Not thine the sense of loss
But lo, for us the void
That never shall be filled again.
Not thine but ours the grief.
All pain is fled from thee.
And we are weeping in thy stead;
Tears for the mourners who are left behind
Peace everlasting for the quiet dead.

LUCRETIUS (99–55 BC)

The Divine Weaver

Our lives are but a weaving
Between our Lord and we;
We cannot choose the colours
He weaves so steadily.
Often He weaves in sorrow
But we in foolish pride
Forget He sees the upper
And we, the lower side.
But the dark threads are as needful
In the weaver's skilful hand
As the threads of gold and silver
In the pattern He has planned.
Not till the loom is silent
And the bobbins cease to fly,
Shall He unroll the canvas
And explain the reason why.

ANON

The Divinity That Stirs Within Us

It must be so. Plato, thou reasonest well!
Else whence this pleasing hope, this fond desire,
This longing after immortality?
Or whence this secret dread, and inward horror
    of falling into naught? Why shrinks the soul
Back on herself, and startles at destruction?
'Tis the divinity that stirs within us.
'Tis Heaven itself that points out an hereafter
    and intimates eternity to man.

TRANSLATION BY JOSEPH ADDISON (1672–1719)
From *Soliloquy on Immortality*

Do Not Go Gentle into That Good Night

Do not go gentle into that good night,
Old age should burn and rave at close of day;
Rage, rage against the dying of the light.

Though wise men at their end know dark is right,
Because their words had forked no lightning they
Do not go gentle into that good night.

Good men, the last wave by, crying how bright
Their frail deeds might have danced in a green bay,
Rage, rage against the dying of the light.

Wild men who caught and sang the sun in flight,
And learn, too late, they grieved it on its way,
Do not go gentle into that good night.

Grave men, near death, who see with blinding sight
Blind eyes could blaze like meteors and be gay,
Rage, rage against the dying of the light.

And you, my father, there on the sad height,
Curse, bless, me now with your fierce tears, I pray.
Do not go gentle into that good night.
Rage, rage against the dying of the light.

DYLAN THOMAS (1914–1953)

Do Not Stand at My Grave and Weep

Do not stand at my grave and weep
I am not there. I do not sleep.
I am a thousand winds that blow.
I am the diamond glints on snow.
I am the sunlight on ripened grain,
I am the gentle autumn rain.
When you awaken in the morning's hush,
I am the swift uplifting rush
Of quiet birds in circled flight.
I am the soft stars that shine at night.
Do not stand at my grave and cry,
I am not there; I did not die.

ANON

Left by Stephen Cummins, a soldier killed in Northern Ireland in
1989

Dying Was Easy

Dying was easy –
Living is hard:
the heart just stopped
and the mind was stilled:
but I am alive
and in protest cry
   'Why?'
Dying was easy –
Living is hard:
you slipped away
when my back was turned;
but I live on
no one answers my sigh
   'Why?'
Dying was easy –
Living is hard:
you are free
but I am bound;
questions need answers
but there are none for me
   'Why?'
Dying was easy –
Living is hard:
but life must go on
for the life we shared.
How I succeed
will make sense of yours –
so no more 'Whys?'

F. FAULKNER (1897–1962)

The End of the Road

When I come to the end of the road
And the sun has set for me
I want no tears in a gloom filled room
Why cry for a soul set free?
Miss me a little, but not too much
And not with your head bowed low
Remember the love that once we shared
Miss me, but let me go
For this is a journey we all must take
And each must go alone
It's all part of God's perfect plan
A step on the road to home
When you are lonely and sick of heart
Go to the friends that we know
And bury your sorrows in doing good
Miss me, but let me go.

ANON

Epitaph on a Child

Here, freed from pain, secure from misery, lies
A child, the darling of his parents' eyes:
A gentler Lamb ne'er sported on the plain,
A fairer flower will never bloom again:
Few were the days allotted to his breath;
Now let him sleep in peace his night of death

THOMAS GRAY (1716–1771)

Epitaph on a Friend

An honest man here lies at rest,
The friend of man, the friend of truth,
The friend of age, and guide of youth:
Few hearts like his, with virtue warm'd,
Few heads with knowledge so inform'd;
If there's another world, he lives in bliss;
If there is none, he made the best of this.

ROBERT BURNS (1759–1796)

Even Such is Time

Even such is time that takes in trust
Our youth, our joys, our all we have,
And pays us but with age and dust,
Who in the dark and silent grave,
When we have wandered all our ways,
Shuts up the story of our days.
But from this earth, this grave, this dust,
My God shall raise me up, I trust.

SIR WALTER RALEIGH (1552–1618)

The Existence of Love

I had thought that your death
Was a waste and a destruction
A pain of grief hardly to be endured.
I am only beginning to learn
That your life was a gift and a growing
And a loving left with me,
That desperation of death
Destroyed the existence of love,
But the fact of death
Cannot destroy what has been given.
I am learning to look at your life again
Instead of your death and your departing.

MARJORIE PIZER (b. 1920)

Farewell

Farewell to Thee! But not farewell
To all my fondest thoughts of Thee;
Within my heart they still shall dwell
And they shall cheer and comfort me.
Life seems more sweet that Thou didst live
And men more true that Thou wert one;
Nothing is lost that Thou didst give,
Nothing destroyed that Thou hast done.

ANNE BRONTË (1820–1847)

Farewell

I have got my leave. Bid me farewell, my brothers!
I bow to you all and take my departure.
Here I give back the keys of my door
– and I give up all claims to my house.
I only ask for last kind words from you.
We were neighbours for long,
but I received more than I could give.
Now the day has dawned
and the lamp that lit my dark corner is out.
A summons has come and I am ready for my journey.

RABINDRANATH TAGORE (1861–1941)

Farewell My Friends

It was beautiful
As long as it lasted
The journey of my life.
I have no regrets
Whatsoever save
The pain I'll leave behind.
Those dear hearts
Who love and care
And the heavy with sleep
Ever moist eyes
The smile in spite of a
Lump in the throat
And the strings pulling
At the heart and soul.
The strong arms
That held me up
When my own strength
Let me down
Each morsel that I was
Fed with was full of love divine.
At every turning of my life
I came across
Good friends
Friends who stood by me
Even when the time raced me by.
Farewell
Farewell

My friends

I smile and

Bid you goodbye

No, shed no tears

For I need them not

All I need is your smile.

If you feel sad

Do think of me

For that's what I'll like

When you live in the hearts

Of those you love

Remember then …

You never die.

RABINDRANATH TAGORE (1861–1941)
From *Gitanjali*

Fear No More the Heat o' the Sun

Fear no more the heat o' the sun
    Nor the furious winter's rages;
Thou thy worldly task has done,
    Home art gone, and ta'en thy wages:
Golden lads and girls all must,
As chimney-sweepers, come to dust.

Fear no more the frown o' the great,
    Thou art past the tyrant's stroke;
Care no more to clothe and eat;
    To thee the reed is as the oak:
The sceptre, learning, physic, must
All follow this, and come to dust.

Fear no more the lightning-flash,
    Nor th'all-dreaded thunder-stone;
Fear not slander, censure rash;
    Thou hast finish'd joy and moan:
All lovers young, all lovers must
Consign to thee, and come to dust.

No exorciser harm thee!
Nor no witchcraft charm thee!
Ghost unlaid forbear thee!
Nothing ill come near thee!
Quiet consummation have;
And renowned be thy grave

WILLIAM SHAKESPEARE (1564–1616)
From *Cymbeline*

Fishing Prayer

God grant that I may live to fish until my dying day,
And when it comes to my last cast then I most humbly pray,
When in the Lord's safe landing net I'm peacefully asleep,
That in His mercy I be judged as good enough to keep.

ANON

Flowers are the Poetry of Christ

For the flowers are great blessings,
For the Lord made a nosegay in the meadow with his disciples
      and preached upon the lily.
For the angels of God took it out of his hand and carried it to
      the Height …
For there is no Height in which there are not flowers.
For flowers have great virtues for all the senses.
For the flower glorifies God and the root parries the adversary.
For the flowers have their angels even the words of God's
      Creation.
For the warp and woof of flowers are working by perpetual
      moving spirits.
For flowers are good both for the living and the dead.
For there is a language of flowers.
For there is a sound reasoning upon all flowers.
For elegant phrases are nothing but flowers.
For flowers are peculiarly the poetry of Christ.

CHRISTOPHER SMART (1722–1771)
From *Rejoice in the Lamb*

Fly, Fly Little Wing

Fly, fly little wing
Fly beyond imagining
The softest cloud, the whitest dove
Upon the wind of heaven's love
Past the planets and the stars
Leave this lonely world of ours
Escape the sorrow and the pain
And fly again.

Fly, fly precious one
Your endless journey has begun
Take your gentle happiness
Far too beautiful for this
Cross over to the other shore
There is peace for ever more
But hold this memory bittersweet
Until we meet.

Fly, fly do not fear
Don't waste a breath, don't shed a tear
Your heart is pure, your soul is free
Be on your way, don't wait for me
Above the universe you'll climb
On beyond the hands of time
The moon will rise, the sun will set
But I won't forget.

Fly, fly little wing
Fly where only angels sing
Fly away the time is right
Go now, find the light

JEAN-JACQUES GOLDMAN and PHIL GALSTON
CD – Celine Dion, *Falling Into You*

For Ben

Eyes that twinkle sunshine,
A face that breaks your heart,
That special look of innocence
Remains while we're apart.
We had you for a short while,
But you brought so many joys,
Now play in peace our baby,
Enjoy your angel toys.
Time will bring us comfort
While waiting for the day
When we will be together again
Not just a whisper away.

ANON

Four Feet

I have done mostly what most men do
And pushed it out of my mind;
But I can't forget if I wanted to
Four feet trotting behind.
Day after day, the whole day through
Wherever my road inclined,
Four feet said 'I'm coming with you'
And trotted along behind.
Now I must go by some other road –
Which I shall never find –
Somewhere that does not carry the sound
Of four feet trotting behind.

RUDYARD KIPLING (1865–1936)

Funeral Blues

Stop all the clocks, cut off the telephone,
Prevent the dog from barking with a juicy bone,
Silence the pianos and with muffled drum
Bring out the coffin, let the mourners come.

Let aeroplanes circle moaning overhead
Scribbling on the sky the message He Is Dead,
Put crepe bows round the white necks of the public doves,
Let the traffic policemen wear black cotton gloves.

He was my North, my South, my East and West,
My working week and my Sunday rest,
My noon, my midnight, my talk, my song;
I thought that love would last forever: I was wrong.

The stars are not wanted now; put out every one,
Pack up the moon and dismantle the sun,
Pour away the ocean and sweep up the woods;
For nothing now can ever come to any good.

    W. H. Auden (1907–1973)

Gaelic Blessing

Deep peace of the running wave to you.
Deep peace of the flowing air to you.
Deep peace of the quiet earth to you.
Deep peace of the shining stars to you.
Deep peace of the gentle night to you.
Moon and stars pour their healing light on you.
Deep peace of Christ, the light of the world to you.
Deep peace of Christ to you.

TRADITIONAL

Gaelic Prayer

May the road rise to meet you,
May the wind be always at your back,
May the sun shine warm upon your face,
May the rains fall softly upon your fields.
Until we meet again,
May God hold you in the hollow of his hand.

TRADITIONAL

The Gate of the Year

I said to the man who stood at the Gate of the Year,
'Give me a light that I may tread safely
into the unknown'.
And he replied,
'Go out into the darkness,
and put your hand into the Hand of God.
That shall be to you better than light
and safer than a known way!'
So I went forth and finding the Hand of God
Trod gladly into the night
He led me towards the hills
And the breaking of day in the lone east.
[So heart be still!
What need our human life to know
If God hath comprehension?
In all the dizzy strife of things
Both high and low,
God hideth his intension.']

MINNIE LOUISE HASKINS (1875–1957)

This poem was read by King George VI in his famous Christmas
speech of 1939, at the beginning of the Second World War. Known
as 'The Gate of the Year', it is the introductory passage to a longer
poem called 'God Knows', found in a collection of works called
The Desert, 1908.

The Glory of the Garden

Our England is a garden that is full of stately views,
Of borders, beds and shrubberies and lawns and avenues,
With statues on the terraces and peacocks strutting by;
But the Glory of the Garden lies in more than meets the eye.

For where the old thick laurels grow, along the thin red wall,
You'll find the tool- and potting-sheds which are the heart of all,
The cold-frames and the hot-houses, the dungpits and the tanks,
The rollers, carts and drain-pipes, with the barrows and the planks.

And there you'll see the gardeners, the men and 'prentice boys
Told off to do as they are bid and do it without noise;
For, except when seeds are planted and we shout to scare the birds,
The Glory of the Garden it abideth not in words.

And some can pot begonias and some can bud a rose,
And some are hardly fit to trust with anything that grows;
But they can roll and trim the lawns and sift the sand and loam,
For the Gory of the Garden occupieth all who come.

Our England is a garden, and such gardens are not made
By singing: – 'Oh, how beautiful!' and sitting in the shade,
While better men than we go out and start their working lives
At grubbing weeds from gravel-paths with broken dinnerknives.

There's not a pair of legs so thin, there's not a head so thick
There's not a hand so weak and white, nor yet a heart so sick,
But it can find some needful job that's crying to be done,
For the Glory of the Garden glorifieth every one.

Then seek your job with thankfulness and work till further orders,
If it's only netting strawberries or killing slugs on borders;
And when your back stops aching and your hands begin to harden,
You will find yourself a partner in the Glory of the Garden.

Oh, Adam was a gardener, and God who made him sees
That half a proper gardener's work is done upon his knees,
So when your work is finished, you can wash your hands and pray
For the Glory of the Garden that it may not pass away!
And the Glory of the Garden it shall never pass away!

RUDYARD KIPLING (1865–1936)

God Called Your Name So Softly

God called your name so softly
That only you could hear
And no-one heard the footsteps
Of angels drawing near
It broke our hearts to lose you
But you did not go alone
For part of us went with you
The day God called you home.

ANON

God Make Me Brave

God make me brave –
Let me strengthen after pain
As a tree strengthens after rain
Shining and lovely again.
As a blown grass lifts, let me rise
From sorrow with quiet eyes
Knowing Thy way is wise
God make me braver – life brings
Such blinding things!
Help me keep Thee in my sight
That out of dark – comes light.

ANON

God of the Open Air

These are the things I prize
And hold of dearest worth:
Light of the sapphire skies,
Peace of the silent hills,
Shelter of forests, comfort of the grass,
Music of birds, murmur of little rills,
Shadow of clouds that swiftly pass,
And, after showers,
The smell of flowers
And of the good brown earth –
And best of all, along the way, friendship and mirth.

So let me keep
These treasures of the humble heart
In possession, owning them by love;
And when at last I can no longer move
Among them freely, but must part
From the green fields and from the waters clear,
Let me not creep
Into some darkened room and hide
From all that makes the world so bright and dear;
But throw the windows wide
To welcome in the light;
And while I clasp a well-loved hand,
Let me once more have sight
Of the deep sky and the far-smiling land –
Then gently fall on sleep,
And breathe my body back to Nature's care,
My spirit out to thee, God of the open air.

HENRY VAN DYKE (1852–1933)
From *God of the Open Air*

God Saw You Getting Tired

God saw you getting tired
When a cure was not to be,
He wrapped his arms around you
And whispered 'Come to me.'
You didn't deserve what you went through,
So He gave you rest.
God's garden must be beautiful,
He only takes the best
And when I saw you sleeping
So peaceful and free from pain
I could not wish you back
To suffer that again
So keep your arms around her, Lord,
And give her special care,
Make up for all she suffered
And all that seemed unfair.

ANON

God's Garden

God looked around his garden
and found an empty space.
Then he looked down upon the earth
and saw your tired face.
He put his arms around you
and lifted you to rest.
God's garden must be beautiful
for He only takes the best.
He knew that you were suffering.
He knew you were in pain.
He knew you never would get well
upon this earth again.
He saw the roads were getting rough
and the hills were hard to climb,
So he closed your weary eyes
and whispered 'Peace be thine'.
It broke my heart to lose you
But you did not go alone
For part of me went with you
the day God called you home.

ANON

The Golden Chain of Friendship

Friendship is a Golden Chain,
The links are friends so dear,
And like a rare and precious jewel
It's treasured more each year ...
It's clasped together firmly
With a love that's deep and true,
And it's rich with happy memories
And fond recollections, too ...
Time can't destroy its beauty
For, as long as memory lives,
Years can't erase the pleasure
That the joy of friendship gives ...
For friendship is a priceless gift
That can't be bought or sold,
But to have an understanding friend
Is worth far more than gold ...
And the Golden Chain of Friendship
Is a strong and blessed tie
Binding kindred hearts together
As the years go passing by.

ANON

Had I the Heaven's Embroidered Cloths

Had I the heaven's embroidered cloths,
Enwrought with golden and silver light,
The blue and the dim and the dark cloths
Of night and light and the half light,
I would spread the cloths under your feet:
But I, being poor, have only my dreams;
I have spread my dreams under your feet;
Tread softly because you tread on my dreams.

W.B. YEATS (1865–1939)

I Don't Believe in Death

I don't believe in death
Who mocks in silent stealth
He robs us only of a breath,
Not of a life-time's wealth.
I don't believe the tomb
Imprisons us in earth;
It's but another loving womb preparing our new birth.
I do believe in Life
Empowered from above;
Till, freed from stress and worldly strife,
We soar through realms above.
I do believe that then, in joy that never ends,
We'll meet all those we've loved, again,
And celebrate our friends.

PAULINE WEBB

I Go, Sweet Friends!

I go, sweet friends! yet think of me
When spring's young voice awakes the flowers;
For we have wandered far and free
In those bright hours, the violet's hours.
I go; but when you pause to hear
From distant hills the Sabbath-bell
On summer-winds float silvery clear.
Think on me then – I loved it well!
Forget me not around your hearth.
When cheerily smiles the ruddy blaze;
For dear hath been its evening mirth
To me, sweet friends, in other days.
And oh! when music's voice is heard
To melt in strains of parting woe,
When hearts to love and grief are stirred,
Think of me then! I go, I go!

ANON

I Have Seen Death Too Often

I have seen death too often
To believe in death:
For it is like arriving at the end of the day,
Turning off the engine, switching off the lights,
And gently closing the car door;
Then walking along the path, up to the steps
And into the light of home.

ANON

I Only Wanted You

They say memories are golden,
Well maybe that is true,
I never wanted memories,
I only wanted you.
A million times I needed you,
A million times I cried,
If love alone could have saved you
You never would have died.
In life I love you dearly,
In death I love you still.
In my heart you hold a place
No one could ever fill.
If tears could build a stairway
And heartache make a lane,
I'd walk the path to heaven
And bring you back again.
Our family chain is broken,
And nothing seems the same.
But as God calls us one by one,
The chain will link again.

ANON

I Was Loved, Therefore I Am

I was loved, therefore I am;
And in being loved, I am treasured.
When I peeled away my layers,
And all that was left was my essence,
The bareness of me,
I was still loved.
I was loved, therefore I am;
And in being loved I was able to grow.
In my mistakes held,
In my successes celebrated,
I was always loved.
I was loved, therefore I am;
And in being loved I learned to love.
In the sun filled day,
In the ecstasy of the night,
I was loved and loved others.
To be loved is all you need:
I was loved … and so, I will always be.

ANA DRAPER

I Would Be True

I would be true for there are those who trust me
I would be pure for there are those who care
I would be strong for there is much to suffer
I would be brave for there is much to dare
I would be friend to all, the foe, the friendless
I would be giving and forget the gift
I would be humble, for I know my weakness
I would look up, and laugh, and love, and live.

ANON

If

If you can keep your head when all about you
Are losing theirs and blaming it on you,
If you can trust yourself when all men doubt you,
But make allowance for their doubting too;
If you can wait and not be tired of waiting,
Or being lied about, don't deal in lies,
Or being hated, don't give way to hating,
And yet don't look too good, nor talk too wise:

If you can dream – and not make dreams your master;
If you can think – and not make thoughts your aim;
If you can meet with Triumph and Disaster
And treat those two impostors just the same;
If you can bear to hear the truth you've spoken
Twisted by knaves to make a trap for fools,
Or watch the things you gave your life to, broken,
And stoop and build 'em up with worn-out tools:

If you can make one heap of all your winnings
And risk it on one turn of pitch-and-toss,
And lose, and start again at your beginnings
And never breathe a word about your loss;
If you can force your heart and nerve and sinew
To serve your turn long after they are gone,
And so hold on when there is nothing in you
Except the Will which says to them: 'Hold on!'

If you can talk with crowds and keep your virtues,
Or walk with Kings – nor lose the common touch,
If neither foes nor loving friends can hurt you,
If all men count with you, but none too much;
If you can fill the unforgiving minute
With sixty seconds' worth of distance run,
Yours is the Earth and everything that's in it,
And – which is more – you'll be a Man, my son!

RUDYARD KIPLING (1865–1936)

If I Be the First of Us to Die

If I be the first of us to die,
Let grief not blacken long your sky.
Be bold yet modest in your grieving.
There is a change but not a leaving.
For just as death is part of life,
The dead live on forever in the living.
And all the gathered riches of our journey,
The moments shared, the mysteries explored,
The steady layering of intimacy stored,
The things that made us laugh or weep or sing,
The joy of sunlit snow or first unfurling of the spring,
The wordless language of look and touch,
The knowing,
Each giving and each taking,
These are not flowers that fade,
Nor trees that fall and crumble,
Nor are they stone,
For even stone cannot the wind and rain withstand
And mighty mountain peaks in time reduce to sand.
What we were, we are.
What we had, we have.
A conjoined past imperishably present.
So when you walk the woods where once we walked together
And scan in vain the dappled bank beside you for my shadow,
Or pause where we always did upon the hill to gaze across the
land,
And spotting something, reach by habit for my hand,
And finding none, feel sorrow start to steal upon you,
Be still.
Close your eyes.
Breathe.
Listen for my footfall in your heart.
I am not gone but merely walk within you.

Nicholas Evans
From *The Smoke Jumper*

If I Should Die and Leave You Here Awhile

If I should die and leave you here awhile,
Be not like others sore undone, who keep
Long vigils by silent dust, and weep.
For my sake, turn again to life and smile,
Nerving thy heart and trembling hand to do
Some thing to comfort weaker hearts than thine
Complete these dear unfinished tasks of mine.
And I, perchance may therein comfort you!

> A. PRICE HUGHES
> Also attributed to Mary Lee Hall. Read at the funeral of Diana,
> Princess of Wales

If I Should Go Tomorrow

If I should go tomorrow
It would never be goodbye,
For I have left my heart with you,
So don't you ever cry.
The love's that's deep within me,
Shall reach you from the stars,
You'll feel it from the heavens,
And it will heal the scars.

> TRADITIONAL

If I Should Never See the Moon Again

If I should never see the moon again
Rising red gold across the harvest fields,
Or feel the stinging of soft April rain,
As the brown earth her bidden treasures yields.
If I should never taste the salt sea spray
As the ship beats her course against the breeze,
Or smell the dog rose and the new-mown hay,
Or moss and primrose beneath the trees.
If I should never hear the thrushes wake
Long before sunrise in the glimmering dawn,
Or watch the huge Atlantic rollers break
Against the rugged cliffs in baffling scorn.
If I have said goodbye to stream and wood,
To the wide ocean and the green clad hill,
I know that He who made this world so good
Has somewhere made a Heaven better still.
This bear I witness with my latest breath.
Knowing the love of God, I fear not death.

MAJOR MALCOLM BOYLE (d. 1944)
The poem was written after D-Day, 6 June 1944, by Major Malcolm
Boyle, of the Green Howards, who was killed in action in
Normandy on 16 June 1944, to his great friend, Captain E.B.
Cottingham MC, Gloucester Regiment.

I'm Free

Don't grieve for me, for now I'm free,
I'm following the path God has laid, you see.
I took his hand when I heard his call
I turned my back and left it all,
I could not stay another day
To laugh, to love, to work, to play
Tasks left undone must stay that way
I found the peace at close of day.
If my parting has left a void
Then fill it with remembered joys –
A friendship shared, a laugh, a kiss
Oh yes! These things I too will miss.
Be not burdened with times of sorrow.
I wish you the sunshine of tomorrow.
My life's been full, I savoured much,
Good friends, good times, a loved one's touch.
Perhaps my time seemed all too brief
Don't lengthen it now with undue grief.
Lift up your hearts, and peace to thee –
God wanted me now, he set me free.

ANON

In Memoriam

With you a part of me hath passed away;
For in the peopled forest of my mind
A tree made leafless by this wintry wind
Shall never don again its green array.
Chapel and fireside, country road and bay,
Have something of their friendliness resigned;
Another, if I would, I could not find,
And I am grown much older in a day.
But yet I treasure in my memory
Your gift of charity, and young heart's ease,
And the dear honour of your amity;
For these once mine, my life is rich with these.
And I scarce know which part may greater be –
What I keep of you, or you rob from me.

GEORGE SANTAYANA (1863–1952)

In Remembrance

You gave me life
To live as I please,
You gave me love and
Support to follow my dreams.
Your beauty lives
Forever deep in my soul,
The memory of your love
Fills my heart
And I am never alone.

CHRISTINE CURRAH, 2002

Into That Heaven of Freedom

Where the mind is without fear and the head is held high;

Where knowledge is free;

Where the world has not been broken up into fragments by
narrow domestic walls;

Where words come out from the depth of truth;

Where tireless striving stretches its arms towards perfection;

Where the clear stream of reason has not lost its way into the
dreary desert sand of dead habit;

Where the mind is led forward by thee into ever-widening
thought and action –

Into that heaven of freedom, my Father, let my country awake.

RABINDRANATH TAGORE (1861–1941)
From *Gitanjali*

A Knight There Was

A knight there was, and that a worthy man,
Who, from the moment when he first began
To ride forth, loved the code of chivalry;
Honour and truth, freedom and courtesy:
Renowned he was; and worthy, he was wise –
Prudence with him was more than mere disguise;
He was meek in manner as a maid
Vileness he shunned, rudeness he never said
In all his life, respecting each man's right
He was a truly perfect, noble knight.

GEOFFREY CHAUCER (1343–1400)
From *The Canterbury Tales*

Kontakion for the Departed

Give rest O Christ to your servant with your saints,
where sorrow and pain are no more,
neither sighing, but life everlasting.
Creator and Maker of humankind, you only are immortal,
and we are mortal, formed of the earth,
and to the earth we shall return:
for so you did ordain when you created us, saying,
Dust thou art and unto dust thou shalt return.
All we go down to the dust,
and, weeping o'er the grave, we make our song:
Alleluia, alleluia, alleluia.
Give rest O Christ to your servant with your saints,
Where sorrow and pain are no more,
Neither sighing, but life everlasting.

ANON

(A kontakion is a Russian prayer)

Life Goes On

If I should go before the rest of you,
Break not a flower nor inscribe a stone.
Nor when I'm gone speak in a Sunday voice,
But be the usual selves that I have known.
Weep if you must,
Parting is hell,
But life goes on,
So sing as well.

JOYCE GRENFELL (1910–1979)
From *Joyce: by Herself and Her Friends*

The Loom of Time

Man's life is laid in the loom of time
To a pattern he does not see,
While the weavers work and the shuttles fly
Till the dawn of eternity.
Some shuttles are filled with silver threads
And some with threads of gold,
While often but the darker hues
Are all that they may hold.
But the weaver watches with skilful eye
Each shuttle fly to and fro,
And sees the pattern so deftly wrought
As the loom moves sure and slow.
God surely planned the pattern:
Each thread, the dark and fair,
Is chosen by His master skill
And placed in the web with care.
He only knows its beauty,
And guides the shuttles which hold
The threads so unattractive,
As well as the threads of gold.
Not till each loom is silent,
And the shuttles cease to fly,
Shall God reveal the pattern
And explain the reason why
The dark threads were as needful
In the weaver's skilful hand
As the threads of gold and silver
For the pattern which He planned.

ANON

Lord, I Come Before You

Lord, I come before you
like a broken vessel,
Dreams shattered, hopes unrealised;
Earthly loving unjustly ended;
Irreplaceable loss imbued with fear;
Conflicting feelings tossed
inwardly.
The pain of separation briefly assuaged
by myriad prayers and love,
surrounding.
Come to me, Man of Sorrows.
Lift me from the darkness of my grief
to the light of your Presence.
Help me to entrust [name]
into the arms of your Eternal Love,
Where suffering ceases and all is well.
Let the Peace which you alone can give
Fill my being
as, with love and thanksgiving,
I give back to you
a life,
which remains now and always
part of my own.

JOHN WYNBURNE

Loss

Something's dead inside me.
Some yesterday is slain.
My heart is hung upon a cross,
my thoughts are dull with pain.
And yet there is within me
a hope I can't explain
For in the darkness I can see
God dancing in the rain.
I surrender to the mystery
of loss that turns to fain.
The little seed of wheat must die
to become a field of grain,
and I know it's in this time of grief,
that Christ is risen again
For in the darkness I can see
God dancing in the rain.

JOY COWLEY (b. 1936)

Love Doesn't End with Dying

Love doesn't end with dying
Or leave with the last breath.
For someone you've loved deeply,
Love doesn't end with death.

JOHN ADDEY

Love is This

Love is this
That you lived amongst us these few years
And taught us love.
Love is this
That you died amongst us and helped us
To the source of life.
With all our love
We wish you bon voyage.
Love lives.

LINDY HEMMY

May Time Soften Your Pain

In times of darkness, love sees …
In times of silence, love hears …
In times of doubt, love hopes …
In times of sorrow, love heals …
And in all times, love remembers.
May time soften the pain
Until all that remains
Is the warmth of the memories
And the love.

ANON

My Life Closed Twice Before Its Close

My life closed twice before its close

It yet remains to see

If Immortality unveils

A third event to me

So huge, so hopeless to conceive

As these that twice befell.

Parting is all we know of heaven,

And all we need of hell.

EMILY DICKENSON (1830–1886)

My True Love Hath My Heart

My true-love hath my heart, and I have his,

    By just exchange one for another given:

I hold his dear, and mine he cannot miss,

    There never was a better bargain driven.

    My true-love hath my heart, and I have his,

My heart in me keeps him and me in one,

    My heart in him his thoughts and senses guide:

He loves my heart, for once it was his own,

    I cherish his because in me it bides.

    My true-love hath my heart, and I have his.

SIR PHILIP SIDNEY (1554–1586)

The Next Place

The next place that I will go will be as peaceful as a sleepy
       summer Sunday
and a sweet untroubled mind.
And yet … it won't be anything like any place I've ever been
       … or seen …
or dreamed of in the place I leave behind…
I won't remember getting there. Somehow I'll just arrive.
But I'll know that I'll belong there and will feel much more
       alive
than I have ever felt before.
I will be absolutely free of things that I held on to that were
       holding on to me…
Though I'll know the joy of solitude, I'll never be alone.
I'll be embraced by all the family and friends I've ever known.
Although I might not see their faces all our hearts will beat as
       one
and the circle of our spirits will shine brighter than the sun.
I will cherish all the friendship I was fortunate to find, all the
       love and all the laughter
in the place I leave behind.
All these good things will go with me. They will make my
       spirit glow.
That light will shine forever … in the next place that I go.

ANON

Not How Did He Die

Not how did he die, but how did he live?
Not what did he gain, but what did he give?
These are the units to measure the worth
Of a man as a man, regardless of birth.
Not what was his church or what was his creed?
But had he befriended those really in need?
Not what was his station, but had he a heart?
How did he play his God-given part?
Was he ever ready, with word of good cheer,
To bring back a smile, to banish a tear?
Not how did the formal obituary run?
But how many grieved when his life's work was done?

ANON

Nothing for Tears

Nothing is here for tears, nothing to wail
Or knock the breast; no weakness, no contempt,
Dispraise or blame; nothing but well and fair
And what may quiet us in a death so noble.

JOHN MILTON (1608–1674)
From *Samson Agonistes*

Old Men Forget

'Old men forget!' aye it may well be so:
But youth remembers all the magic spun
and woven in the warm fraternal glow
of your companionship. Your day is done?
It is not true. You know you left behind
a memory of courage which the years
can but increase. And we, your heirs, will find
that in good truth there's nothing here for tears.
So be it. This your legacy to youth –
to make the best of all your days
and finally to recognise the truth
and you have shown us, silhouetted, stark
that though we love the sunlight's summer rays
we need not fear the coming of the dark.

STANLEY OF ALDERLEY

On Another's Sorrows

Can I see another's woe
And not be in sorrow too?
Can I see another's grief
And not seek for kind relief?

Can I see a falling tear
And not feel my sorrows share?
Can a father see his child,
Weep, nor be with sorrow fill'd?

Can a mother sit and hear
An infant groan, an infant fear?
No, no! never can it be, never!
Never, never can it be!

And can He who smiles on all
Hear the wren with sorrows small,
Hear the small bird's grief and care,
Hear the woes that infants bear,

And not sit beside the nest
Pouring pity in their breast;
And not sit the cradle near,
Weeping tear on infant's tear;

And not sit both night and day,
Wiping all our tears away?
O no! never can it be!
Never, never can it be!

He doth give his joy to all;
He comes an infant small;
He becomes a man of woe;
He doth feel the sorrow too.

Think not thou canst sigh a sigh,
And thy Maker is not by;
Think not thou canst weep a tear,
And thy Maker is not near.

O! He gives to us his joy
That our grief He may destroy;
Till our grief is fled and gone
He doth sit by us and moan.

WILLIAM BLAKE (1757–1827)

On Parting With a Friend

Can I forget thee? No, while mem'ry lasts,
Thine image like a talisman entwined,
Around my heart by sacred friendship's ties
Remains unchanged, in love, pure love, enshrined.

Can I forget thee? Childhood's happy hours
Would like some flitting phantom mock and jeer;
Life's sunny hours, would quickly lose their charm,
If Lethe's slumberous waves but touched me there.

Can I forget thee? 'Tis a sad, sad thought,
That friend from friend should thus be ruthless riven –
But list, methinks, a sweet voice whispers low,
Remember, no adieus are spoken in heaven.

Can I forget thee? No, though ocean's waves
May madly leap and foam 'twixt you and me,
Still o'er my stricken heart this yearning will remain,
Nor time estrange my love, dear one, from thee.

And though on earth again we never more may meet,
In that bright Elysian where spirits, holy, dwell,
May we in concert with that transported throng,
Unite, ne'er more (rapt thought) to say 'farewell!'

MARY WESTON FORDHAM (b. 1862)

Our Little Life Is Rounded with a Sleep

Our revels are now ended. These our actors,
As I foretold you, were all spirits, and
Are melted into air, into thin air:
And, like the baseless fabric of this vision,
The cloud-capp'd towers, the gorgeous palaces,
The solemn temples, the great globe itself,
Yea all which it inherit, shall dissolve,
And, like this insubstantial pageant faded,
Leave not a rack behind. We are such stuff
As dreams are made on; and our little life
Is rounded with a sleep.

WILLIAM SHAKESPEARE (1564–1616)
From *The Tempest*

Paradise: In a Dream

Once in a dream I saw the flowers
    That bud and bloom in Paradise;
    More fair they are than waking eyes
Have seen in all this world of ours.
And faint the perfume-bearing rose,
    And faint the lily on its stem,
And faint the perfect violet
      Compared with them.
I heard the songs of Paradise:
    Each bird sat singing in his place;
    A tender song so full of grace
It soared like incense to the skies.
Each bird sat singing to his mate
    Soft cooing notes among the trees:
The nightingale herself were cold
      To such as these.
I saw the fourfold River flow,
    And deep it was, with golden sand;
    It flowed between a mossy land
Which murmured music grave and low.
It hath refreshment for all thirst,
    For fainting spirits strength and rest:
Earth holds not such a draught as this
      From east to west.
The Tree of Life stood budding there,
    Abundant with its twelvefold fruits;
    Eternal sap sustains its roots,
Its shadowing branches fill the air.
Its leaves are healing for the world,
    Its fruit the hungry world can feed,
Sweeter than honey to the taste
      And balm indeed.

I saw the gate called Beautiful;
    And looked, but scarce could look, within;
    I saw the golden streets begin,
And outskirts of the glassy pool.
Oh harps, oh crowns of plenteous stars,
    Oh green palm-branches many-leaved –
Eye hath no seen, nor ear hath heard,
        Nor heart conceived.
I hope to see these things again,
    But not as once in dreams by night;
    To see them with my very sight,
And touch, and handle, and attain:
To have all Heaven beneath my feet
    For narrow way that once they trod;
To have my part with all the Saints,
        And with my God.

CHRISTINA ROSSETTI (1830–1894)

The Parting Glass

Of all the time that e'er I spent,
I spent it in good company,
and any harm that e'er I've done,
I trust it was to none but me.
May those I've loved through all the years
have mem'ries now they e'er recall.
So fill to me the parting glass;
Goodnight and joy be with you all.
Of all the comrades that e'er I had
are sorry for my going away
and all the loved ones that e'er I had
would wish me one more day to stay,
but since it falls unto my lot
that I should leave and you should not
I'll gently rise and I'll softly call
Goodnight and joy be with you all.
Of all good times that e'er we shared
I leave to you fond memory,
and for all the friendship that e'er we had
I ask you to remember me,
and when you sit and stories tell,
I'll be with you and help recall.
So fill to me the parting glass
God bless and joy be with you all.

IRISH TRADITIONAL SONG

Perhaps

Perhaps, if we could see
    The splendour of the land
    To which our loved are called from you and me
    We'd understand.
Perhaps, if we could hear
    The welcome they receive
    From old familiar voices – all so dear –
    We would not grieve.
Perhaps, if we could know
    The reason why they went
    We'd smile – and wipe away the tears that flow
    And wait content.

ANON

Poem for James

One day my world fell apart;
The beginning became an end,
The dawn, the dusk.
In blank incomprehension dreams
once dreamt were short-lived
and hopes turned to despair.
A blow knocked my life out of shape.
A sword pieced my heart.
Numbed by senseless reality,
mangled and tortured emotions
could find no words.
Questions chased around in my head,
halted by respite only from the
deep sobs of my aching heart.
Annunciation had heralded joy and fear,
leading to quiet acceptance and
peaceful anticipation of a new creation
– so beautifully and wonderfully made –
a gift growing, nourished within.
In agonizing hours of naked
vulnerability,
past, present and future were
transformed –
sinking into the depths of darkness.
What might have been
in this earthly bundle of bright
beautiful innocence

faded to the silence of eternity

and the song of the angels –

A light of joy extinguished here,

rekindled there –

and part of me went too.

The ripples of devastation spread

Engulfing all with sadness.

Fragile faith became yet more

Interrogative

behind irrepressible grief,

and exhausted body and numbed spirit.

Surrounded by those who care,

enfolded by those who love,

upheld by invisible hands,

strengthened by prayerful voices,

a beam of light proffered a healing

balm for all wounds.

And through the prism of my tears

I saw again the Love that moves the

Sun and other stars

that whisper gently to my grieving

Heart –

'yes, all IS well'.

JOHN WYNBURNE
Written after a neonatal death

The Prayer of St Francis

Lord, make me an instrument of your peace.

Where there is hatred, let me sow love.

Where there is injury, pardon.

Where there is doubt, faith.

Where there is despair, hope.

Where there is darkness, light.

Where there is sadness, joy.

O, Divine Master, grant that I may not so much seek

To be consoled, as to console;

To be understood, as to understand;

To be loved, as to love;

For it is in giving that we receive,

It is in pardoning that we are pardoned,

And it is in dying that we are born to eternal life.

ST FRANCIS OF ASSISI (C. 1181–1226)

Regret Not Me

Regret not me;
Beneath the sunny tree
I lie uncaring, slumbering peacefully.

Swift as the light
I flew my faery flight;
Ecstatically I moved, and feared no might.

I did not know
That heydays fade and go,
But deemed that what was would be always so.

I skipped at morn
Between the yellowing corn,
Thinking it good and glorious to be born.

I ran at eves
Among the piled-up sheaves,
Screaming, 'I grieve not, therefore nothing grieves.'

Now soon will come
The apple, pear, and plum,
And hinds will sing, and autumn insects hum.

Again you will fare
To cider-makings rare,
And junketings; but I shall not be there.

Yet gaily sing
Until the pewter ring
Those songs we sang when we went gipsying.

And lightly dance
Some triple-timed romance
In coupled figures and forget mischance;

And mourn not me
Beneath the yellowing tree;
For I shall mind not, slumbering peacefully.

THOMAS HARDY (1840–1928)

Remember

Remember me when I am gone away,
Gone far away into the silent land;
When you can no more hold me by the hand,
Nor I half turn to go yet turning stay.
Remember me when no more day by day
You tell me of our future that you plann'd:
Only remember me: you understand
It will be late to counsel then or pray.
Yet if you should forget me for a while
And afterwards remember, do not grieve:
For if the darkness and corruption leave
A vestige of the thought that once I had,
Better by far you should forget and smile
Than that you should remember and be sad.

CHRISTINA ROSSETTI (1830–1894)

Remember Me

Remember me when I am gone
But not with sorrow, pain and grief
Think of me as a turning leaf
That in the Winter falls from its branch
To be born again in Spring
And live forever in your heart.

CHRISTINE CURRAH, 2002

Remembering

You can shed tears that he is gone
    Or you can smile because he has lived.
You can close your eyes and pray that he'll come back
    Or you can open your eyes and see all he's left.
Your heart can be empty because you can't see him
    Or you can be full of the love you shared.
You can turn your back on tomorrow and live yesterday
    Or you can be happy for tomorrow because of yesterday.
You can remember him and only that he has gone
    Or you can cherish his memory and let it live on.
You can cry and close your mind, be empty and turn your back
    Or you can do what he'd want: smile, open your eyes,
        love and go on.

ANON

Requiem

Under the wide and starry sky
Dig the grave and let me lie:
Glad did I live and gladly die,
And I laid me down with a will

This be the verse you grave for me:
Here he lies where he long'd to be;
Home is the sailor, home from the sea,
And the hunter home from the hill.

ROBERT LOUIS STEVENSON (1850–1894)

The Rich and the Poor Listen to the Voice of Death

The rich and the poor listen to the voice of death;
The learned and the unlearned listen;
The proud and the humble listen;
The honest and deceitful listen;
The old and the young listen.
But when death speaks to us, what does it say?
Death does not speak about itself.
It does not say 'Fear me'.
It does not say, 'Wonder at me'.
It does not say 'Understand me'.
But it says to us:
'Think of life;
Think of the privilege of life;
Think how great a thing life may be made.'

ANON

The Rose Beyond the Wall

Near shady wall a rose once grew,
Budded and blossomed in God's free light,
Watered and fed by morning dew,
Shedding its sweetness day and night.
As it grew and blossomed fair and tall,
Slowly rising to loftier height,
It came to a crevice in the wall,
Through which there shone a beam of light.
Onward it crept with added strength,
With never a thought of fear or pride;
It followed the light through the crevices length
And unfolded itself on the other side.
The light, the dew, the broadening view
Were found the same as they were before;
And it lost itself in beauties new,
Breathing its fragrance more and more.
Shall claim of death cause us to grieve
And make our courage faint or fail?
Nay! Let us faith and hope receive;
The rose still grows beyond the wall.
Scattering fragrance far and wide,
Just as it did in the days of yore,
Just as it did on the other side,
Just as it will forever more.

ALMIRA L. FRINK (b. 1870)

Safely Home

I am at home in heaven, dear ones;
Oh, so happy and so bright!
There is perfect joy and beauty
In this everlasting light.
All the pain and grief is over
Every restless tossing passed:
I am now at peace for ever
Safely home in heaven at last.
Did you wonder I so calmly
Trod the valley of the shade?
Oh! But Jesus' love illumined
Every dark and fearful glade.
And he came himself to meet me
In the way so hard to tread
And with Jesus' arm to lean on
Could I have one doubt or dread?
Then you must not grieve so sorely
For I love you dearly still,
Try to look beyond earth's shadows
Pray to trust our Father's will.
There is work still waiting for you,
So you must not idly stand
Do it now, while life remaineth –
You shall rest in Jesus' hand.
When the work is all completed,
He will gently call you home
Oh, the rapture of that meeting,
Oh, the hope to see you come!

ANON

Sarum Prayer

God be in my head, and in my understanding.

God be in my eyes, and in my looking.

God be in my mouth, and in my speaking.

God be in my heart, and in my thinking.

God be at my end, and at my departing.

TRADITIONAL

Sea Fever

I must go down to the seas again, to the lonely sea and the sky,
And all I ask is a tall ship and a star to steer her by,
And the wheel's kick and the wind's song and the white sail's
        shaking,
And a grey mist on the sea's face and a grey dawn breaking.
I must go down to the seas again, for the call of the running
        tide
Is a wild call and a clear call that may not be denied;
And all I ask is a windy day with the white clouds flying,
And the flung spray and the blown spume and the seagulls
        crying.
I must go down to the seas again to the vagrant gypsy life.
To the gull's way and the whale's way where the wind's like a
        whetted knife:
And all I ask is a merry yarn from a laughing fellow-rover,
And quiet sleep and a sweet dream when the long trick's over.

JOHN MASEFIELD (1878–1967)

The Soldier

If I should die, think only this of me;
That there's some corner of a foreign field
That is for ever England. There shall be
In that rich earth a richer dust concealed,
A dust whom England bore, shaped, made aware,
A body of England's breathing English air
Washed by rivers, blessed by sons of home.

And think, this heart, all evil shed away,
A pulse in the eternal mind, no less
Gives somewhere back the thoughts by England given,
Her sights and sounds, dreams happy as her day,
And laughter, learnt of friends, and gentleness,
In hearts at peace, under an English heaven.

RUPERT BROOKE (1887–1915)

Song

When I am dead, my dearest,
Sing no sad songs for me;
Plant thou no roses at my head,
Nor shady cypress tree:
Be the green grass above me
With showers and dewdrops wet;
And if thou wilt, remember,
And if thou wilt, forget.

I shall not see the shadows,
I shall not feel the rain;
I shall not hear the nightingale
Sing on, as if in pain;
And dreaming through the twilight
That doth not rise nor set;
Haply I may remember;
And haply may forget.

CHRISTINA ROSSETTI (1830–1894)

Sonnet for Zuleika and Bega Who Kept Watch

We know about death – we dogs do know about death
For us there's no mystery, because we understand
In our hearts, in our bones, in our every breath
That all must cross that grey and ashen land.
We grieve and watch although we cannot weep.
There are no tears, no words to shape our pain.
With quiet respect we wait and silent keep
Our vigil – knowing we'd fight with death in vain.
This life we've shared is part of all we are,
A lasting space of ease and simple love.
The fun, walks, our hols, or dins, the car
The riotous games that threatened 'retribution from above'
And grief lasts not forever. We too must die.
In time we'll turn our heads and softly pass by.

LUCY JACKSON

Sonnet XXX

When to the sessions of sweet silent thought
    I summon up remembrance of things past,
I sigh the lack of many a thing I sought,
    And with old woes new wail my dear time's waste:
Then can I drown an eye, unused to flow,
    For precious friends hid in death's dateless night,
And weep afresh love's long since cancelled woe,
    And moan the expense of many a vanished sight:
Then can I grieve at grievances forgone,
    And heavily from woe to woe tell o'er,
The sad account of fore-bemoanèd moan,
    Which I new pay as if not paid before.
        But if the while I think on thee, dear friend,
        All losses are restored and sorrows end.

WILLIAM SHAKESPEARE (1564–1616)

The Sparrow's Prayer

Father, before this sparrow's earthly flight
Ends in the darkness of a winter's night;
Father, without whose words no sparrow falls,
Hear this, Thy weary sparrow, when he calls.
Mercy, not justice, is his contrite prayer,
Cancel his guilt and drive away despair;
Speak but the word, and make his spirit whole,
Cleanse the dark places of his heart and soul.
Speak but the word, and set his spirit free;
Mercy, not justice, still his constant plea.
So shall Thy sparrow, crumpled wings restored,
Soar like a lark, and glorify his Lord.

LORD HAILSHAM (1907–2001)

There

There, in that other world, what waits for me?
What shall I find after that other birth?
No stormy, tossing, foaming, smiling sea,
But a new earth.
No sun to mark the changing of the days,
No slow, soft falling of the alternate night,
No moon, no star, no light upon my ways,
Only the Light.
No grey cathedral, wide and wondrous fair,
That I may tread, where all my fathers trod.
Nay, nay, my soul, no house of God is there,
But only God.

MARY COLERIDGE (1861–1907)

There Is No Indispensable Man

Sometimes when you're feeling important;
Sometime when your ego's in bloom
Sometime when you take it for granted
You're the best qualified in the room,
Sometime when you feel that your going
Would leave an unfillable hole,
Just follow these simple instructions
And see how they humble your soul;
Take a bucket and fill it with water,
Put your hand in it up to the wrist,
Pull it out and the hole that's remaining
Is a measure of how you'll be missed.
You can splash all you wish when you enter,
You may stir up the water galore,
But stop and you'll find that in no time
It looks quite the same as before.
The moral of this quaint example
Is do just the best that you can,
Be proud of yourself but remember,
There is no indispensable man.
And yet there's a Man up in Heaven
Without whom each man lives in vain;
Through we can dispense with all others
He's the one indispensable Man.
He came into the world to save sinners
And no other man could do this,
From Earth to Heaven's glorious bliss
We can do without this one or that one,
It's quite easy to soon fill their place;
But to do without Christ means disaster,
With a life gone to ruin and waste.
The moral of this is quite simple
Take Christ as your saviour and Friend
Then you'll see him one day up in Heaven
Where joys know no measure nor end.

ANON

A Thing of Beauty Is a Joy Forever

A thing of beauty is a joy forever:
Its loveliness increases; it will never
Pass into nothingness; but still will keep
A bower quiet for us, and a sleep
Full of sweet dreams, and health, and quiet breathing.
Therefore, on every morrow, are we wreathing
A flowery band to bind us to the earth,
Spite of despondence, of the inhuman dearth
Of noble natures, of the gloomy days,
Of all the unhealthy and o'er-darkened ways
Made for our searching: yes, in spite of all,
Some shape of beauty moves away the pall
From our dark spirits. [Such the sun, the moon,
Trees old, and young, sprouting a shady boon
For simple sheep; and such are daffodils
With the green world they live in; and clear rills
That for themselves a cooling covert make
'Gainst the hot season; the mid-forest brake,
Rich with a sprinkling of fair musk-rose blooms
And such too is the grandeur of the dooms
We have imagined for the mighty dead;
All lovely tales that we have heard or read –
And endless fountain of immortal drink
Pouring into us from the heaven's brink.]

JOHN KEATS (1795–1821)
From *Endymion*

This Heritage

They are not dead,
Who leave us this great heritage
Of remembered joy.
They still live in our hearts,
In the happiness we knew,
In the dreams we shared.
They still breathe,
In the lingering fragrance windblown,
From their favourite flowers.
They still smile in the moonlight's silver
And laugh in the sunlight's sparkling gold.
They still speak in the echoes of words
We've heard them say again and again.
They still move,
In the rhythm of waving grasses,
In the dance of the tossing branches.
They are not dead;
Their memory is warm in our hearts,
Comfort in our sorrow.
They are not apart from us,
But a part of us
For love is eternal,
And those we love shall be with us
Throughout all eternity.

ANON

Though I Am Dead

Though I am dead, grieve not for me with tears,
Think not of death with sorrowing and fears,
I am so near that every tear you shed
Touches and tortures me, though you think me dead …
But when you laugh and sing in glad delight,
My soul is lifted upwards to the Light:
Laugh and be glad for all that Life is giving,
And I though dead will share your joy of living.

ANON

The Tide Recedes

The tide recedes, but leaves behind
Bright seashells on the sand.
The sun goes down but gentle warmth
Still lingers on the land.
The music stops and yet it lingers on
In sweet refrain.
For every joy that passes
Something beautiful remains.

M. D. HUGHES

Time

Time is ...

    Too Slow for those who Wait,
    Too Swift for those who Fear,
    Too Long for those who Grieve,
    Too Short for those who Rejoice,
But for those who Love,
    Time is Eternity.

    ANON

'Tis Better to Have Loved and Lost

I envy not in any moods
The captive void of noble rage,
The linnet born within the cage,
That never knew the summer woods:
I envy not the beast that takes
His license in the field of time,
Unfetter'd by the sense of crime,
To whom a conscience never wakes;
Nor, what may count itself as blest,
The heart that never plighted troth
But stagnates in the weeds of sloth,
Nor any want-begotten rest.
I hold it true, whate'er befall;
I feel it when I sorrow most;
'Tis better to have loved and lost
Than never to have loved at all.

ALFRED, LORD TENNYSON (1809–1892)
From *In Memoriam*

To a Loved One

I'll think of thee, mine own, dear one
As morn's first blushing ray
Diffuses light o'er the dim earth –
Turns darkness into day.
I'll think of thee at eve, my love,
When moon and star appear –
When in the horizon of my hope
All, all is bright and clear.
I'll think of thee when joy doth cast
Its gladness o'er my heart,
As peace, and love and happiness
Seem new life to impart.
I'll think of thee when dark shades fall
Athwart my fevered brow;
When low in death I hear thee lisp –
'I'm waiting for thee now.'
I'll think of thee, my darling one,
While I have life and breath;
And seal the assurance fervently,
I'll think of thee in death.

MARY WESTON FORDHAM (b. 1862)

Trailing Clouds of Glory

Our birth is but a sleep and a forgetting:
The soul that rises with us, our life's Star
Hath had elsewhere its setting,
And cometh from afar:
Not in entire forgetfulness,
And not in utter nakedness,
But trailing clouds of glory do we come
From God, who is our home:
Heaven lies about us in our infancy!

WILLIAM WORDSWORTH (1770–1850)
From *Intimations of Immortality*

Up Hill

Does the road wind up-hill all the way?
    Yes, to the very end.
Will the day's journey take the whole long day?
    From morn to night, my friend.
But is there for the night a resting-place?
    A roof for when the slow dark hours begin.
May not the darkness hide it from my face?
    You cannot miss that inn.
Shall I meet other wayfarers at night?
    Those who have gone before.
Then must I knock. Or call when just in sight?
    They will not keep you standing at the door.
Shall I find comfort, travel-sore and weak?
    Of labour you shall find the sum.
Will there be beds for me and all who seek?
    Yes, beds for all who come.

CHRISTINA ROSSETTI (1830–1894)

When I Am Gone

When I am gone release me,
Let me go, I have so many things to see and do.
You mustn't tie yourself to me with tears,
Be happy that we had so many beautiful years.
I gave to you my love.
You can only guess how much you gave me in happiness.
I thank you for the love you each have shown,
But now it's time I travel alone.
So grieve awhile for me, if grieve you must,
Then let your grief be comforted by my trust.
It's only for a while that we must part,
So bless the memories within your heart.
I won't be far away, for life goes on,
So if you need me, call and I will come.
Though you can't see or touch me, I'll be near.
And if you listen within your heart you'll hear
All my love around you soft and clear.
And then when you must come this way alone
I'll greet you with a smile and say
'Welcome Home.'

ANON

When I Die

When I die
Give what's left of me away,
To children
And those that wait to die.
And if you need to cry,
Cry for your brother
Walking the street beside you.
And when you need me,
Put your arms
Around anyone
And give them
What you need to give me.
I want to leave you something,
Something better
Than words
Or sounds.
Look for me
In the people I've known
Or loved.
And if you cannot give me away,
At least let me live in your eyes
And not in your mind.
You can love me most
By letting
Hands touch bodies,
And by letting go
Of children
That need to be free.
Love doesn't die,
People do.
So, when all that's left of me
Is love,
Give me away

ANON

When I Have Fears

When I have fears, as Keats had fears,
Of the moment I'll cease to be
I console myself with vanished years
Remembered laughter, remembered tears,
And the peace of the changing sea.
When I feel sad, as Keats felt sad
That my life is so nearly done
It gives me comfort to dwell upon
Remembered friends who are dead and gone
And the jokes we had and the fun.
How happy they are I cannot know,
But happy am I who loved them so.

NOËL COWARD (1899–1973)

When we are Weary and in Need of Strength

When we are weary and in need of strength,

When we are lost and sick at heart,

We remember him.

When we have a joy we crave to share,

When we have decisions that are difficult to make,

When we have achievements that are based on his,

We remember him.

At the blowing of the wind and in the chill of winter,

At the opening of the buds and in the rebirth of spring,

We remember him.

At the blueness of the skies and in the warmth of summer,

At the rustling of the leaves and in the beauty of autumn,

We remember him.

At the rising of the sun and at its setting,

We remember him.

As long as we live, he too will live,

For he is now a part of us,

As we remember him.

Adapted from *The Yizkor Service, Jewish Funeral Service Prayer Book*

When You Are Old

When you are old and grey and full of sleep,
And nodding by the fire, take down this book,
And slowly read, and dream of the soft look
Your eyes had once, and of their shadows deep;

How many loved your moments of glad grace,
And loved your beauty with love false or true,
But one man loved the pilgrim soul in you,
And loved the sorrows of your changing face;

And bending down beside the glowing bars,
Murmur, a little sadly, how Love fled
And paced upon the mountains overhead
And hid his face amid a crowd of stars.

W.B. YEATS (1865–1939)

Yes, Thou Art Gone!

Yes, thou art gone! And never more
Thy sunny smile shall gladden me;
But I may pass the old church door,
And pace the floor that covers thee,
May stand upon the cold, damp stone,
And think that, frozen, lies below
The lightest heart that I have known,
The kindest I shall ever know.

Yet, though I cannot see thee more,
'Tis still a comfort to have seen;
And though thy transient life is o'er,
'Tis sweet to think that thou hast been;

To think a soul so near divine,
Within a form, so angel fair,
United to a heart like thine,
Has gladdened once our humble sphere.

ANNE BRONTË (1820–1849)

You Touched My Life

You touched my life
And turned my heart around.
It seems when I found you
It was me I really found.
You opened my eyes
And now my soul can see
Our moments may be over,
Of just you here with me.
Love lives on beyond Goodbye
The truth of us will never die.
Our spirits will shine
Long after we've gone,
And so our love lives on.
There was so much
I didn't understand
When you brought me here
Far from where we all began.
The changes you made
To my life will never end.
I'll look across the distance
And know I have a friend.
Love lives on beyond Goodbye
The truth of us will never die
Our spirits will shine
Long after we've gone,
And so our love lives on.
And so our love lives on.

ANON

You'll Never Walk Alone

When you walk through the storm
Hold your head up high,
And don't be afraid of the dark.
At the end of the storm
Is a golden sky
And the sweet silver song of a lark.
Walk on through the wind,
Walk on through the rain,
Though your dreams be tossed and blown.
Walk on, walk on with hope in your heart
And you'll never walk alone.
You'll never walk alone.

OSCAR HAMMERSTEIN (1846–1919)
From *Carousel*

BIBLE READINGS

Not everyone will want to use readings from the Bible, but there is a great deal of comfort and solace to the bereaved to be found in the Scriptures. These have been chosen from the version of the Bible that seemed most apposite. Many of these readings are given in the exquisite old English of the King James Version but, for some of the more popular and familiar ones, a modern alternative has also been included for those who feel it would be more appropriate to their loved one and the occasion.

OLD TESTAMENT READINGS

By His Wounds We are Healed

Who has believed our message and to whom has the arm of the Lord been revealed?

He grew up before him like a tender shoot, and like a root out of dry ground. He had no beauty or majesty to attract us to him, nothing in his appearance that we should desire him. He was despised and rejected by men, a man of sorrows, and familiar with suffering. Like one from whom men hide their faces he was despised and we esteemed him not.

Surely he took up our infirmities and carried out sorrows, yet we considered him stricken by God, smitten by him, and afflicted. But he was pierced for our transgressions, he was crushed for our iniquities; the punishment that brought us peace was upon him, and by his wounds we are healed.

ISAIAH 53: 1–11

Do Not Forget There Is No Coming Back

Remember your creator in the days of your youth, before the days of trouble come, and the years draw near when you will say, 'I have no pleasure in them';

before the sun and the light and the moon and the stars are darkened and the clouds return with the rain;

in the day when the guards of the house tremble, and the strong men are bent, and the women who grind cease working because they are few, and those who look through the windows see dimly;

when the doors on the street are shut, and the sound of the grinding is low, and one rises up at the sound of a bird, and all the daughters of song are brought low;

when one is afraid of heights, and terrors are in the road; the almond tree blossoms, the grasshopper drags itself along and desire fails;

because all must go to their eternal home, and the mourners will go about the streets; before the silver cord is snapped, and the golden bowl is broken, and the pitcher is broken at the fountain, and the wheel broken at the cistern, and the dust returns to the earth as it was,

and the breath returns to God who gave it.

ECCLESIASTES 12: 1–7

Finding Strength Through Trust

How lovely is thy dwelling place, O Lord of hosts! My soul longs, yea, faints for the courts of the Lord; my heart and flesh sing for joy to the living God.

Even the sparrow finds a home, and the swallow a nest for herself, where she may lay her young, at thy altars, O Lord of hosts, my King and my God. Blessed are those who dwell in thy house ever singing thy praise!

Blessed are the men whose strength is in thee, in whose heart are the highways to Zion. As they go through the valley of Baca they make it a place of springs; the early rain also covers it with pools. They go from strength to strength; the God of gods will be seen in Zion.

O Lord God of hosts, hear my prayer; give ear, O God of Jacob! Behold our shield, O God; look upon the face of thine anointed!

For a day in thy courts is better than a thousand elsewhere. I would rather be a doorkeeper in the house of my God than dwell in the tents of wickedness. For the Lord God is a sun and shield; he bestows favour and honour. No good thing does the Lord withhold from those who walk uprightly.

O Lord of hosts, blessed is the man who trusts in thee!

PSALM 84

God Is Our Refuge and Strength

God is our refuge and strength, a very present help in trouble. Therefore we will not fear though the earth should change, though the mountains shake in the heart of the sea; though its waters roar and foam, though the mountains tremble with its tumult.

There is a river whose streams make glad the city of God, the holy habitation of the Most High. God is in the midst of the city, it shall not be moved; God will help it when the morning dawns. The nations are in an uproar, the kingdoms totter; he utters his voice, the earth melts. The Lord of hosts is with us; the God of Jacob is our refuge.

Come, behold the works of the Lord, see what desolations he has brought on the earth. He makes wars cease to the end of the earth; he breaks the bow, and shatters the spear; he burns the shields with fire.

'Be still, and know that I am God! I am exalted among the nations, I am exalted in the earth.'

The Lord of hosts is with us; the God of Jacob is our refuge.

Psalm 46

A Good Wife

A good wife who can find? She is far more precious than
jewels.

The heart of her husband trusts in her, and he will have no
lack of gain. She does him good, and not harm, all the
days of her life.

She seeks wool and flax, and works with willing hands. She
girds her loins with strength and makes her arms
strong. She opens her hand to the poor, and reaches out
her hands to the needy.

Strength and dignity are her clothing, and she laughs at the
time to come. She opens her mouth with wisdom, and
the teaching of kindness is on her tongue. She looks well
to the ways of her household, and does not eat the bread
of idleness. Her children rise up and call her blessed; her
husband also, and he praises her:

'Many women have done excellently, but you surpass them all.'

PROVERBS 31: 10–13, 17, 20, 25–29

Great Is God's Faithfulness

The steadfast love of the Lord never ceases, his mercies never come to an end; they are new every morning; great is your faithfulness.

'The Lord is my portion,' says my soul, 'therefore I will hope in him.'

The Lord is good to those who wait for him, to the soul that seeks him. It is good that one should wait quietly for the salvation of the Lord.

For the Lord will not reject forever. Although he cause grief, he will have compassion according to the abundance of his steadfast love; for he does not willingly afflict or grieve anyone.

LAMENTATIONS 3: 22–26, 31–33

Hope in God

As the deer pants for streams of water, so my soul pants for you, O God. My soul thirsts for God, for the living God. When can I go and meet with God? My tears have been my food day and night, while men say to me all day long, 'Where is your God?'

Why are you downcast, O my soul? Why so disturbed within me? Put your hope in God, for I will yet praise him, my Saviour and my God.

By day the Lord directs his love, at night his song is with me – a prayer to the God of my life.

PSALM 42: 1–3, 5, 8

I Know That My Redeemer Lives

Oh, that my words were recorded, that they were written on a scroll, that they were inscribed with an iron tool on lead, or engraved in rock forever!

I know that my Redeemer lives, and that in the end he will stand upon the earth. And after my skin has been destroyed, yet in my flesh I will see God; I myself will see him with my own eyes – I, and not another.

How my heart yearns within me!

JOB 19: 23–27

I Lift Up My Eyes to the Hills

I lift up my eyes to the hills – where does my help come from?
My help comes from the Lord, the Maker of heaven and earth.
> He will not let your foot slip – he who watches over you
> will not slumber; indeed, he who keeps Israel will
> neither slumber nor sleep.
The Lord watches over you – the Lord is your shade on your
> right hand; the sun will not harm you by day, nor the
> moon by night.
The Lord will keep you from all harm – he will watch over
> your life; the Lord will watch over your coming and
> going both now and for evermore.

PSALM 121

I Will Lift Up Mine Eyes unto the Hills

I will lift up mine eyes unto the hills, from whence cometh my
help. My help cometh from the Lord which made
heaven and earth.

He will not suffer thy foot to be moved: he that keepeth thee
will not slumber. Behold, he that keepeth Israel shall
neither slumber nor sleep. The Lord is thy keeper: the
Lord is thy shade upon thy right hand.

The sun shall not smite thee by day, nor the moon by night.
The Lord shall preserve thee from all evil: he shall
preserve thy soul. The Lord shall preserve thy going out
and thy coming in from this time forth, and even for
evermore.

PSALM 121

The Lord God Will Wipe Away Tears from All Faces

He will swallow up death for ever, the Lord God will wipe
away tears from all faces, and the reproach of his people he will
take away from all the earth; for the Lord has spoken.

It will be said on that day, 'Lo, this is our God; we have waited
for him, that he might save us. This is the Lord; we have
waited for him; let us be glad and rejoice in his salvation.'

Thou dost keep him in perfect peace, whose mind is stayed on
thee, because he trusts in thee. Trust in the Lord for ever, for
the Lord God is an everlasting rock.

ISAIAH 25: 8–9, 26:3–4

The Lord Is My Light and My Salvation

The Lord is my light and my salvation – whom shall I fear?
The Lord is the stronghold of my life – of whom shall I be
afraid? When evil men advance against me to devour my flesh,
when my enemies and my foes attack me, they will stumble
and fall. Though an army besiege me, my heart will not fear;
though war break out against me even then will I be confident.

One thing I ask of the Lord, this is what I seek: that I may
dwell in the house of the Lord all the days of my life, to gaze
upon the beauty of the Lord and to seek him in his temple. For
in the day of trouble he will keep me safe in his dwelling; he
will hide me in the shelter of his tabernacle and set me high
upon a rock.

I am still confident of this: I will see the goodness of the
Lord in the land of the living. Wait for the Lord; be strong and
take heart and wait for the Lord.

PSALM 27: 1–5, 13–14

The Lord Is My Shepherd

The Lord is my shepherd, I shall not want. He maketh me to lie down in green pastures; he leadeth me beside the still waters. He restoreth my soul: he leadeth me in the paths of righteousness for his name's sake.

Yea, though I walk through the valley of the shadow of death, I will fear no evil: for thou art with me; thy rod and thy staff they comfort me.

Thou preparest a table before me in the presence of mine enemies: thou anointest my head with oil; my cup runneth over.

Surely goodness and mercy shall follow me all the days of my life: and I will dwell in the house of the Lord for ever.

PSALM 23

The Lord Is My Shepherd

The Lord is my shepherd, I shall not want. He makes me lie down in green pastures, he leads me beside quiet waters, he restores my soul. He guides me in paths of righteousness for his name's sake.

Even though I walk through the valley of the shadow of death, I will fear no evil, for you are with me; your rod and your staff, they comfort me.

You prepare a table before me in the presence of my enemies. You anoint my head with oil; my cup overflows.

Surely goodness and love will follow me all the days of my life, and I will dwell in the house of the Lord for ever.

PSALM 23

Lord, You Have Been Our Dwelling Place in All Generations

Lord, thou hast been our dwelling place in all generations. Before the mountains were brought forth, or ever thou hadst formed the earth and the world, from everlasting to everlasting thou art God. Thou turnest us back to the dust, and say, 'Turn back, O children of men!'

For a thousand years in thy sight are but as yesterday when it is past, or like a watch in the night. Thou dost sweep men away; they are like a dream, like grass which is renewed in the morning: in the morning it flourishes and is renewed; in the evening it fades and withers.

The years of our life are threescore and ten, or even by reason of strength fourscore; yet their span is but toil and trouble; they are soon gone, and we fly away.

So teach us to number our days that we may gain a heart of wisdom.

PSALM 90: 1–6, 10, 12

O Lord, You Have Searched Me and You Know Me

O Lord, you have searched me and you know me. You know when I sit and when I rise; you perceive my thoughts from afar. You discern my going out and my lying down; you are familiar with all my ways.

Before a word is on my tongue you know it completely, O Lord. You hem me in – behind and before; you have laid your hand upon me. Such knowledge is too wonderful for me, too lofty for me to attain.

Where can I go from your Spirit? Where can I flee from your presence? If I go up to the heavens, you are there; if I make my bed in the depths, you are there. If I rise on the wings of the dawn, if I settle on the far side of the sea, even there your hand will guide me, your right hand will hold me fast.

If I say, 'Surely the darkness will hide me and the light became night around me,' even the darkness will not be dark to you; the night will shine like the day, for darkness is as light to you.

For you created my inmost being; you knit me together in my mother's womb. I praise you because I am fearfully and wonderfully made; your works are wonderful, I know that full well. My frame was not hidden from you when I was made in the secret place. When I was woven together in the depths of the earth, your eyes saw my unformed body. All the days ordained for me were written in your book before one of them came to be.

How precious to me are your thoughts, O God! How vast is the sum of them!

Search me, O God, and know my heart; test me and know my anxious thoughts. See if there is any offensive way in me, and lead me in the way everlasting.

PSALM 139: 1–17, 23–24

Out of the Depths I Cry to You, O Lord

Out of the depths I cry to you, O Lord. Lord, hear my voice! Let your ears be attentive to the voice of my supplications!

If you, O Lord, should mark iniquities, Lord, who could stand? But there is forgiveness with you, so that you may be revered.

I wait for the Lord, my soul waits, and in his word I hope; for with the Lord there is steadfast love, and with him is great power to redeem.

PSALM 130: 1–5, 7B

Praise the Lord

The Lord is merciful and gracious, slow to anger and abounding in steadfast love. He will not always accuse, nor will he keep his anger forever. He does not deal with us according to our sins, not repay us according to our iniquities.

For as the heavens are high above the earth, so great is his steadfast love toward those who fear him; as far as the east is from the west, so far he removes our transgressions from us. As a father has compassion for his children, so the Lord has compassion for those who fear him. For he knows how we were made; he remembers that we are dust.

As for mortals, their days are like grass; they flourish like a flower of the field; for the wind passes over it, and it is gone, and its place knows it no more.

But the steadfast love of the Lord is from everlasting to everlasting on those who fear him, and his righteousness to children's children, to those who keep his covenant and remember to do his commandments.

PSALM 103: 8–18

Safe in God's Hands

The souls of the upright are in the hands of God, and no torment can touch them.

To the unenlightened, they appeared to die, their departure was regarded as disaster, their leaving us like annihilation; but they are at peace. If, as it seemed to us, they suffered punishment, their hope was rich with immortality; slight was their correction, great will their blessings be.

God was putting them to the test and has proved them worthy to be with him; he has tested them like gold in a furnace, and accepted them as a perfect burnt offering. Those who trust in him will understand the truth, those who are faithful will live with him in love; for grace and mercy await his holy ones, and he intervenes on behalf of his chosen.

THE APOCRYPHA
Wisdom of Solomon 3: 1–6, 9

There Is a Time for Everything

For everything there is a season, and a time for every matter under heaven:

a time to be born, and a time to die;

a time to plant, and a time to pluck up what is planted;

a time to kill, and a time to heal;

a time to break down, and a time to build up;

a time to weep, and a time to laugh;

a time to mourn, and a time to dance;

a time to throw away stones, and a time to gather stones together;

a time to embrace, and a time to refrain from embracing;

a time to seek, and a time to lose;

a time to keep, and a time to throw away;

a time to tear, and a time to sew;

a time to keep silence, and a time to speak;

a time to love, and a time to hate;

a time for war, and a time for peace.

What gain have the workers from their toil? I have seen the business that God has given to everyone to be busy with. He has made everything suitable for its time; moreover he has put a sense of past and future into their minds, yet they cannot find out what God has done from the beginning to the end.

I know that there is nothing better for them than to be happy and enjoy themselves as long as they live; moreover, it is God's gift that all should eat and drink and take pleasure in all their toil.

ECCLESIASTES 3: 1–13

To Comfort All Those Who Mourn

The spirit of the Lord God is upon me, because the Lord has
   anointed me;

he has sent me to bring good news to the oppressed, to bind up
   the brokenhearted, to proclaim liberty to the captives,
   and release to the prisoners;

to proclaim the year of the Lord's favour, and the day of
   vengeance of our God;

to comfort all who mourn; to provide for those who mourn in
   Zion – to give them a garland instead of ashes, the oil of
   gladness instead of mourning, the mantle of praise
   instead of a faint spirit.

They will be called oaks of righteousness, the planting of the
   Lord, to display his glory.

ISAIAH 61: 1–3

Value the Services of a Doctor

Value the services of a doctor for he has his place assigned him by the Lord. His skill comes from the Most High, and he is rewarded by Kings. The doctor's knowledge gives him high standing and wins him the admiration of the great. The Lord has created remedies from the earth, and a sensible man will not disparage them. Was not water sweetened by a log, and so the power of the Lord was revealed? The Lord has imparted knowledge to mortals, that by their use of his marvels he may win praise; by means of them the doctor relieves pain and from them the pharmacist compounds his mixture. There is no limit to the works of the Lord, who spreads health over the whole world.

My son, in time of illness do not be remiss, but pray to the Lord and he will hear you. Keep clear of wrongdoing, amend your ways, and cleanse your heart from all sin. Bring a fragrant offering and a memorial sacrifice of flour; pour oil on the sacrifice; be as lavish as you can. And the doctor should be called; keep him by you, for you need him also. A time may come when your recovery is in his hands; then he too will pray to the Lord to grant success in relieving pain and finding a cure to save the patient's life.

ECCLESIASTES 38: 1–14

NEW TESTAMENT READINGS

The Beatitudes

And seeing the multitudes, he went up into a mountain: and
    when he was set, his disciples came unto him: and he
    opened his mouth, and taught them, saying,

Blessed are the poor in spirit: for theirs is the kingdom of
    heaven.

Blessed are they that mourn: for they shall be comforted.

Blessed are the meek: for they shall inherit the earth.

Blessed are they that hunger and thirst after righteousness: for
    they shall be filled.

Blessed are the merciful: for they shall obtain mercy.

Blessed are the pure in heart: for they shall see God.

Blessed are the peacemakers: for they shall be called the
    children of God.

Blessed are they which are persecuted for righteousness' sake:
    for theirs is the kingdom of heaven.

Blessed are ye, when men shall revile you, and persecute you,
    and shall say all manner of evil against you falsely, for
    my sake. Rejoice, and be exceeding glad: for great is
    your reward in heaven.

MATTHEW 5: 1–12A

The Beatitudes

Now when he saw the crowds, he went up on a mountainside
and sat down. His disciples came to him, and he began
to teach them, saying:
Blessed are the poor in spirit, for theirs is the kingdom of
heaven.
Blessed are those who mourn, for they will be comforted.
Blessed are the meek, for they will inherit the earth.
Blessed are those who hunger and thirst for righteousness, for
they will be filled.
Blessed are the merciful, for they will be shown mercy.
Blessed are the pure in heart, for they will see God.
Blessed are the peacemakers, for they will be called the sons of
God.
Blessed are those who are persecuted because of righteousness,
for theirs is the kingdom of heaven.
Blessed are you when people insult you, persecute you and
falsely say all kinds of evil against you because of me.
Rejoice and be glad, because great is your reward in
heaven.

MATTHEW 5: 1–12A

Christ the Lord of the Living and the Dead

We do not live to ourselves, and we do not die to ourselves.
If we live, we live to the Lord, and if we die, we die to the
Lord; so then, whether we live or whether we die, we are the
Lord's.
For to this end Christ died and lived again, so that he might
be Lord of both the dead and the living.

ROMANS 14: 7–9

The Greatest of These Is Love

If I speak in the tongues of men and of angels, but have not love, I am a noisy gong or a clanging cymbal. And if I have the prophetic powers, and understand all mysteries and all knowledge, and if I have all faith, so as to remove mountains, but have not love, I am nothing. If I give away all I have, and if I deliver my body to be burned, but have not love, I gain nothing.

Love is patient, love is kind; love is not jealous, or boastful; it is not arrogant or rude. Love does not insist on its own way; it is not irritable or resentful; it does not rejoice at wrong, but rejoices in the right. Love bears all things, believes all things, hopes all things, endures all things.

Love never ends; as for prophecies, they will pass away; as for tongues, they will cease; as for knowledge, it will pass away. For our knowledge is imperfect and our prophecy is imperfect; but when the perfect comes, the imperfect will pass away.

When I was a child, I spoke like a child, I thought like a child, I reasoned like a child; when I became a man, I gave up childish ways. For now we see in a mirror dimly, but then face to face. Now I know in part; then I shall understand fully, even as I have been fully understood.

So faith, hope and love abide, these three; but the greatest of these is love.

1 Corinthians 13

The Heavenly Body

But we have this treasure in clay jars, so that it may be made clear that this extraordinary power belongs to God and does not come from us.

We are afflicted in every way, but not crushed; perplexed, but not driven to despair; persecuted, but not forsaken; struck down, but not destroyed; always carrying in the body the death of Jesus, so that the life of Jesus may also be made visible in our bodies.

But just as we have the same spirit of faith that is in accordance with scripture – 'I believed, and so I spoke' – we also believe, and so we speak, because we know that the one who raised the Lord Jesus will raise us also with Jesus, and will bring us with you into his presence. Yes, everything is for your sake, so that grace, as it extends to more and more people, may increase thanksgiving, to the glory of God.

So we do not lose heart. Even though our outer nature is wasting away, our inner nature is being renewed day by day. For this slight momentary affliction is preparing us for an eternal weight of glory beyond all measure, because we look not at what can be seen but at what cannot be seen; for what can be seen is temporary, but what cannot be seen is eternal.

2 CORINTHIANS 4: 7–10, 13–18

I Am the Bread of Life

Then Jesus declared, 'I am the bread of life. He who comes to me will never go hungry, and he who believes in me will never be thirsty.

But as I told you, you have seen me and still you do not believe. All that the Father gives me will come to me, and whoever comes to me I will never drive away. For I have come down from heaven not to do my will but to do the will of him who sent me.

And this is the will of him who sent me, that I shall lose none of all that he has given me, but raise them up at the last day. For my Father's will is that everyone who looks to the Son and believes in him shall have eternal life, and I will raise him up at the last day.'

JOHN 6: 35–40

In My Father's House Are Many Rooms

'Let not your heart be troubled: ye believe in God, believe also in me. In my Father's house are many mansions: if it were not so, I would have told you. I go to prepare a place for you. And if I go and prepare a place for you, I will come again, and receive you into myself; that where I am, there you may be also. And whither I go ye know, and the way ye know.'

Thomas saith unto him, 'Lord, we know not whither thou goest; and how can we know the way?'

Jesus saith unto him, 'I am the way, the truth, and the life: no man cometh unto the Father, but by me.

Peace I leave with you, my peace I give unto you: not as the world giveth, give I unto you. Let not your heart be troubled, neither let it be afraid.'

JOHN 14: 1–6, 27

In My Father's House are Many Rooms

'Do not let your hearts be troubled. Believe in God, believe also in me.

In my Father's house there are many dwelling places. If it were not so, would I have told you that I go to prepare a place for you? And if I go and prepare a place for you, I will come again and will take you to myself, so that where I am, there you may be also. And you know the way to the place where I am going.'

Thomas said to him, 'Lord, we do not know where you are going. How can we know the way?'

Jesus said to him, 'I am the way, the truth, and the life. No one comes to the Father except through me.

Peace I leave with you; my peace I give you. I do not give to you as the world gives. Do not let your hearts be troubled, and do not let them be afraid.'

JOHN 14: 1–6, 27

Jesus Blesses the Little Children

People were bringing little children to Jesus to have him touch them, but the disciples rebuked them. When Jesus saw this, he was indignant.

He said to them, 'Let the little children come to me, and do not hinder them, for the kingdom of God belongs to such as these. I tell you the truth, anyone who will not receive the kingdom of God like a little child will never enter it.'

And he took the children in his arms, put his hands on them and blessed them.

MARK 10: 13–16

Jesus the Good Shepherd

Therefore Jesus said again, 'I tell you the truth, I am the gate for the sheep. All who ever came before me were thieves and robbers, but the sheep did not listen to them. I am the gate; whoever enters through me will be saved. He will come in and go out, and find pasture. The thief comes only to steal and kill and destroy; I have come that they may have life, and have it to the full.

My sheep listen to my voice; I know them, and they follow me. I give them eternal life, and they shall never perish; no one can snatch them out of my hand.'

JOHN 10: 7–10, 27–28

A Living Hope

Blessed be the God and Father of our Lord Jesus Christ!
By his great mercy he has given us a new birth into a living hope through the resurrection of Jesus Christ from the dead, and into an inheritance that is imperishable, undefiled, and unfading, kept in heaven for you, who are being protected by the power of God through faith for a salvation ready to be revealed in the last time.

In this you rejoice, even if now for a little while you have had to suffer various trials, so that the genuineness of your faith – being more precious than gold that, though perishable, is tested by fire – may be found to result in praise and glory and honour when Jesus Christ is revealed.

Although you have not seen him, you love him; and even though you do not see him now, you believe in him and rejoice with an indescribable and glorious joy, for you are receiving the outcome of your faith, the salvation of your souls.

1 PETER 1: 3–9

Love and Live at Peace with Everyone

Let love be genuine; hate what is evil, hold fast to what is good; love one another with mutual affection; out do one another in showing honour. Do not lag in zeal, be ardent in spirit, serve the Lord.

Rejoice in your hope, be patient in suffering, persevere in prayer. Contribute to the needs of the saints, extend hospitality to strangers.

Bless those who persecute you; bless and do not curse them. Rejoice with those who rejoice, weep with those who weep. Live in harmony with one another; do not be haughty, but associate with the lowly; do not claim to be wiser than you are.

Do not repay anyone evil for evil, but take thought for what is noble in the sight of all. If it is possible, so far as it depends upon you, live peaceably with all.

Do not be overcome by evil, but overcome evil with good.

ROMANS 12: 9–18

Love One Another as I Have Loved You

As the Father has loved me, so have I loved you; abide in my love.

If you keep my commandments, you will abide in my love, just as I have kept my Father's commandments and abide in his love. I have said these things to you so that my joy may be in you, and that your joy may be complete.

This is my commandment, that you love one another as I have loved you. No one has greater love than this, to lay down one's life for one's friends.

You are my friends if you do what I command you. I do not call you servants any longer, because the servant does not know what the master is doing; but I have called you friends, because I have made known to you everything that I have heard from my Father.

You did not choose me, but I chose you. And I appointed you to go and bear fruit, fruit that will last, so that the Father will give you whatever you ask him in my name.

I am giving you these commands so that you may love one another.

JOHN 15: 9–17

The Multitude from Every Nation

After this I looked, and there was a great multitude that no one could count, from every nation, from all tribes and peoples and languages, standing before the throne and before the Lamb, robed in white, with palm branches in their hands. They cried out in a loud voice, saying, 'Salvation belongs to our God who is seated on the throne, and to the Lamb!'

And all the angels stood around the throne and around the elders and the four living creatures, and they fell on their faces before the throne and worshipped God, singing, 'Amen! Blessing and glory and wisdom and thanksgiving and honour and power and might be to our God forever and ever! Amen.'

Then one of the elders addressed me, saying, 'Who are these, robed in white, and where have they come from?'

I said to him, 'Sir, you are the one that knows.'

Then he said to me, 'These are they who have come out of the great ordeal; they have washed their robes and made them white in the blood of the Lamb. For this reason they are before the throne of God and worship him day and night within his temple, and the one who is seated on the throne will shelter them. They will hunger no more, and thirst no more; the sun will not strike them, nor any scorching heat; for the Lamb at the centre of the throne will be their shepherd, and he will guide them to springs of the water of life, and God will wipe away every tear from their eyes.'

REVELATION 7: 9–17

The New Heaven and the New Earth

And I saw a new heaven and a new earth: for the first heaven and the first earth were passed away; and there was no more sea. And I saw the holy city, new Jerusalem, coming down from God out of heaven, prepared as a bride adorned for her husband. And I heard a great voice out of heaven saying,

'Behold, the tabernacle of God is with men, and he will dwell with them, and they shall be his people, and God himself shall be with them, and be their God. And God shall wipe away all tears from their eyes; and there shall be no more death, neither sorrow, not crying, neither shall there be any more pain: for the former things are passed away.'

And he that sat upon the throne said, 'Behold, I make all things new.'

And he said unto me, 'Write: for these words are true and faithful.'

And he said unto me, 'It is done.

I am Alpha and Omega, the beginning and the end. I will give unto him that is athirst of the fountain of the water of life freely. He that overcometh shall inherit all things; and I will be his God, and he shall be my son.'

REVELATION 21: 1–7

Nothing Can Separate Us from the Love of God

I consider that the sufferings of this present time are not worth comparing with the glory about to be revealed to us. We know that all things work together for good for those who love God, who are called according to his purpose.

Who shall separate us from the love of Christ? Will hardship, or distress, or persecution, or famine, or nakedness, or peril or sword?

As it is written: 'For your sake we are being killed all day long; we are accounted as sheep to be slaughtered.'
No, in all these things we are more than conquerors through him who loved us. For I am convinced that neither death nor life, nor angels nor rulers, nor things present, nor things to come, nor powers, nor height, nor depth, nor anything else in all creation, will be able to separate us from the love of God in Christ Jesus our Lord.

ROMANS 8: 18, 28, 35A–39

The Power to Understand Christ's Love

For this reason I bow my knees before the Father, from whom every family in heaven and on earth takes its name. I pray that, according to the riches of his glory, he may grant that you may be strengthened in your inner being with power through his Spirit, and that Christ may dwell in your hearts through faith, as you are being rooted and grounded in love.

I pray that you may have the power to comprehend, with all the saints, what is the breadth and length and height and depth, and to know the love of Christ that surpasses knowledge, so that you may be filled with all the fullness of God.

Now to him who by the power at work within us is able to accomplish abundantly far more than all we can ask or imagine, to him be glory in the church and in Christ Jesus to all generations forever and ever. Amen.

EPHESIANS 3: 14–21

The Raising of Lazarus

When Jesus arrived, he found that Lazarus had already been in the tomb four days. Now Bethany was near Jerusalem, some two miles away, and many of the Jews had come to Martha and Mary to console them about their brother.

When Martha heard that Jesus was coming, she went and met him, while Mary stayed at home. Martha said to Jesus, 'Lord, if you had been here, my brother would not have died. But even now I know that God will give you whatever you ask of him.'

Jesus said to her, 'Your brother will rise again.'

Martha said to him, 'I know that he will rise again in the resurrection on the last day.'

Jesus said to her, 'I am the resurrection and the life. Those who believe in me, even though he die, will live, and everyone who lives and believes in me will never die. Do you believe this?'

She said to him, 'Yes, Lord, I believe that you are the Messiah, the Son of God, the one coming into the world.'

JOHN 11: 17–27

Rejoice in the Lord Always

Rejoice in the Lord always; again I will say, Rejoice.
Let your gentleness be known to everyone. The Lord is near.
Do not worry about anything, but in everything by prayer and
supplication with thanksgiving let your requests be made
known to God.

And the peace of God, which surpasses all understanding,
will guard your hearts and your minds in Christ Jesus.

Finally, beloved, whatever is true, whatever is honourable,
whatever is just, whatever is pure, whatever is pleasing,
whatever is commendable, if there is any excellence and if
there is anything worthy of praise, think about these things.

Keep doing the things that you have learned and received
and heard and seen in me, and the God of peace will be with
you.

PHILIPPIANS 4: 4–9

The Resurrection

On the first day of the week, very early in the morning, the women took the spices they had prepared and went to the tomb. They found the stone rolled away from the tomb, but when they entered, they did not find the body of the Lord Jesus.

While they were wondering about this, suddenly two men in clothes that gleamed like lightening stood beside them. In their fright the women bowed down with their faces to the ground, but the men said to them,

'Why do you look for the living among the dead? He is not here; he has risen! Remember how he told you, while he was still with you in Galilee: "The Son of Man must be delivered into the hands of sinful men, be crucified and on the third day be raised again."'

Then they remembered his words.

LUKE 24: 1–8

The Resurrection of the Body

If in this life only we have hoped in Christ, we are of all people most to be pitied. But in fact Christ has been raised from the dead, the first fruits of those who have died. For since death came through a human being, the resurrection of the dead has also come through a human being; for as all die in Adam, so all will be made alive in Christ.

But someone will ask, 'How are the dead raised? With what kind of body do they come?' Fool! What you sow does not come to life unless it dies. And as for what you sow, you do not sow the body that is to be, but a bare seed, perhaps of wheat or of some other grain. But God gives it a body as he has chosen, and to each kind of seed its own body.

So it is with the resurrection of the dead. What is sown is perishable, what is raised is imperishable. It is sown in dishonour, it is raised in glory. It is sown in weakness, it is raised in power. It is sown a physical body, it is raised a spiritual body. If there is a physical body, there is also a spiritual body.

[For this perishable body must put on imperishability, and this mortal body must put on immortality. When this perishable body puts on imperishability, and this mortal body puts on immortality, then the saying that is written will be fulfilled:

'Death has been swallowed up in victory.'

'Where, O death, is your victory? Where, O death is your sting?'

But thanks be to God, who gives us the victory through our Lord Jesus Christ. Therefore, my beloved, be steadfast, immovable, always excelling in the work of the Lord, because you know that in the Lord your labour is not in vain.]

1 CORINTHIANS 15: 19–22, 35–38, 42–44, [53–55, 57–58]

Who Is the Greatest in the Kingdom of Heaven?

At that time the disciples came to Jesus and asked, 'Who is the greatest in the kingdom of heaven?'

He called a little child and had him stand among them. And he said: 'I tell you the truth, unless you change and become like little children, you will never enter the kingdom of heaven. Therefore, whoever humbles himself like this child is the greatest in the kingdom of heaven. And whoever welcomes a little child like this in my name welcomes me.'

'See that you do not look down on one of these little ones. For I tell you that their angels in heaven always see the face of my Father in heaven.'

MATTHEW 18: 1–5, 10

You Have Been Raised to Life in Christ

If then you have been raised with Christ, seek the things that are above, where Christ is, seated at the right hand of God. Set your minds on things that are above, not on things that are on earth.

For you have died, and your life is hid with Christ in God. When Christ who is our life appears, then you also will appear with him in glory.

Put on then, as God's chosen ones, holy and beloved, compassion, kindness, lowliness, meekness, and patience, forbearing one another and, if one has a complaint against another, forgiving each other; as the Lord has forgiven you, so you also must forgive.

And above all these put on love, which binds everything together in perfect harmony. And let the peace of Christ rule in your hearts … And be thankful.

COLOSSIANS 3: 1–4, 12–15

MUSIC FOR FUNERALS

Music has great power to touch us at a deep level. At certain times it can express that which words alone may not. It can connect with our thoughts and emotions and 'speak' to us. The choice of music for a funeral can be very important and significant, conveying the variety of feelings that will often accompany the death of a loved one. Specific music or songs can bring back special memories of people, places and experiences that we shall treasure. When the right music and the right words are combined, the effect can be very powerful and moving; tears may flow unexpectedly. Music evokes both sad and happy feelings, so as well as giving comfort to those who mourn, it can also lift up our spirits and give us encouragement and hope.

Some people know very little music and few or no hymns; others will be knowledgeable and have clear ideas. If you are thinking about music you might like at your own funeral, leaving suggestions can be helpful to those who will make the final arrangements. However, as always, it is important to add the proviso 'if possible' because, for various reasons, it may not be possible to carry out your wishes precisely and those left do not want an added burden of guilt.

If you are choosing music for a loved one, you will naturally want to give thought as to whether there are pieces of music, hymns or songs that were special to them. You may be aware of musical pieces that you know meant a great deal to them. However, it is often the case that no favourite music comes to mind. This should not cause concern. Others around you may have ideas or the minister or person conducting the funeral should be able to help choose appropriate music. Although few funerals take place without any music at all, even if it is just played at the beginning and at the end of the service, it is important not to feel you are 'letting down' anybody if you opt for the minimum.

Most crematoria now have quite sophisticated music systems that offer a huge range and choice of music which can be provided at the press of a button. Generally, the provision of music is becoming more mechanised but the quality can still be extremely good whether it is instrumental or to accompany singing. An organist is also usually available as many people still prefer to have 'live' music played.

CDs

Crematoria also have facilities for playing your own CD tracks and most churches and other dedicated religious buildings can also play music from a CD. This allows you to play music that may be of another style or is simply not suitable for a traditional instrument such as a piano or organ.

It is important to check with the funeral director that this facility is available where the funeral is taking place. Sometimes you may be encouraged to do a test run (especially in a church) to make sure that everything operates smoothly. Sometimes you may be asked to transfer the appropriate track on to a separate CD. This reduces the chance of an unsuitable track being played by accident. Your public library should have a copy of *The Gramophone Classical Catalogue (Master Edition)*, which may help you to locate recordings of music you do not have. It is not always necessary to play the whole of a piece of music; it can be stopped or faded out as seems appropriate to you.

Choosing the Music

A funeral service will often include a variety of music:

- quiet and reflective
- solid and traditional
- joyful, uplifting and celebratory

The minister or person leading the service will be glad to discuss with you what hymns or other music you would like, what is most suitable for the occasion and what expresses your feelings. A person arranging a funeral who has little or no knowledge about music is often happy to entrust the choice to the minister or another. It is not easy, especially when in the midst of grief or shock to think about these matters yourself; very often the mind goes blank when you are asked to make suggestions. But you do not have to make decisions about every detail – you will be dealing with professional people who will seek to provide what is best and most helpful for you. They will know all the favourite pieces of music, hymns and songs that down the years have often been used because they seem to connect with the feelings people have on such an occasion.

Hymns

It is usual to have two or three hymns, but there are no hard and fast rules. When choosing hymns:

- check that the tune you want and know is the one you wish to have; some hymns have more than one tune
- omit a verse or more when the hymn is long, time is short or the words are unsuitable
- choose hymns that people are likely to know or at least be familiar with
- let the number of hymns you choose be influenced by the number of people likely to be present and the time available; generally speaking, a service in church offers more time than a service at a crematorium chapel but some of the latter are now giving more generous 'slots'
- be aware that a reasonably up-beat, triumphant hymn at the end helps to lift people's spirits, though you don't have to take this option – it is a matter of personal choice

A list of hymns has been included to help you (see pages 329–31). They should be fairly familiar to most people and can be found in *Hymns Ancient and Modern Revised, New Hymns and Worship Songs, Mission Praise, Hymns Old and New* or *Songs of Fellowship*.

Other Music

Music is generally played either on the organ, from a CD or via a music system while people enter and wait for the service to begin and when leaving. Very often a special piece is chosen at the time when a coffin is brought in and when it is carried out of the building.

Sometimes music is played during a time of quiet reflection, for example after an address or tribute or before a prayer.

A selection of appropriate music has been given as a guide (see pages 331–4) and there are also websites that may be useful.

Choirs and Soloists

A choir, when available, can greatly enhance the singing and help to make the service special. Many churches have choirs, though its members are usually less available during the week. However, it is always worth asking. Depending on the level of ability, special anthems or pieces sung by the choir can bring a distinctive quality to the service. There is usually a modest charge for a church choir.

Alternatively, there are professional singers or choirs that can be 'hired' for the occasion. The local organist can usually advise or look for advertisements in your local music shop or library.

In addition to a choir or as an alternative, a solo performance can be very moving.

Bells

Many churches in this country have a peal of bells. It is less common now than in years past to ring bells for a funeral but it does happen. When bells are rung at a funeral, they are often 'half-muffled'. If not the full peal of bells, the tolling of a single bell as the coffin arrives and/or leaves can be memorable and poignant. If you like the idea, do ask whether the bells might be available.

Piper
The pipes are traditionally played in Scotland and Ireland and the sound can be very moving. Occasionally, people will engage a piper who will play before or after the service, particularly to lead the coffin out of the church.

Suggestions for Hymns
Abide with me
All creatures of our God and King
All people that on earth do dwell
All things bright and beautiful
Alleluia! Sing to Jesus!
Amazing grace
As pants the hart for cooling streams
As the deer pants for the water
Battle hymn of the republic
Be still, for the presence of the Lord, the Holy One is here
Be still, my soul: the Lord is on thy side
Be thou my vision, O Lord of my heart
Blest are the pure in heart
Christ, whose glory fills the skies
Dear Lord and Father of mankind
Eternal Father, strong to save
Fight the good fight
Firmly I believe and truly
For all the saints who from their labours rest
Glorious things of thee are spoken
God be in my head, and in my understanding
Great is thy faithfulness
Guide me, O thou great Redeemer
He who would valiant be
Hills of the north rejoice

How sweet the name of Jesus sounds
I am the Bread of Life
I vow to thee, my country
I would be true, for there are those that trust me
Immaculate Mary! Our hearts are on fire
Immortal, Invisible, God only wise
In heavenly love abiding
Jerusalem, Jesus lives
Jesu, lover of my soul
Jesus, remember me (Taizé)
Just as I am, without one plea
Lead us, heavenly Father, lead us
Lead kindly light
Let all the world in every corner sing
Lord of all hopefulness
Lord of the dance
Love divine, all loves excelling
Love's redeeming work is done
Make me a channel of thy peace
Morning has broken
My soul, there is a country
My song is love unknown
Nearer my God to Thee
Now thank we all our God
O God, our help in ages past
O Jesus I have promised
O Lord my God, when I in awesome wonder
O love that wilt not let me go
O worship the King all glorious above
Onward Christian soldiers
Praise, my soul, the King of heaven
Praise to the Holiest in the height
Praise to the Lord, the Almighty, the King of creation
Rock of ages, cleft for me
Tell out, my soul, the greatness of the Lord

The day thou gavest, Lord, is ended
The Church's one foundation
The King of love my shepherd is
The Lord's my Shepherd, I'll not want
The old rugged cross
The strife is o'er
There is a green hill far away
Thine be the glory, risen, conquering son
To God be the glory, great things he has done
When I survey the wondrous Cross

Suggestions for Organ Music

Albinoni	Adagio
Bach	Sheep May Safely Graze
	Air (from Suite No. 3 in D)
	8 Short Preludes
	Jesu, Joy of Man's Desiring
	Prelude No. 1
	Toccata and Fugue in D minor
Bach/Gounod	Prelude No. 1/Ave Maria
Elgar	Nimrod (from Enigma Variations)
	The Ascent of Angels (from The Dream of Gerontius)
Fauré	Go Forth Upon Thy Journey
	From Requiem:
	In Paradisum
	Pie Jesu
Frank	Panis Angelicus
Guilmant	Organ Sonatas (Slow movements)
Handel	Largo
	Selections from Water Music
	From The Messiah:
	Hallelujah Chorus
	He Shall Feed His Flock Like a Shepherd
	I Know That My Redeemer Liveth

Lefébure-Wély	Sortie in E flat
Mendelssohn	I Waited For The Lord
Mozart	Ave Verum Corpus
Pachelbel	Canon in D
Widor	Toccata from Symphony No. 5
Wright	Brother James' Air – 23rd Psalm

Various arrangements of Ave Maria
Various arrangements of The Lord Is My Shepherd

Less Traditional Choices for Organ Music

Bach	Bist du bei mir (Blessed Jesu, We Are Here) (chorale prelude)
	Chorale preludes, fugues and fantasias
	Adagio from Toccata, Adagio and Fugue in C
Elgar	Chanson d'Amour
Fauré	Pavane
Handel	Selections from the Firework Music
	Where E'er You Walk
Walton	Crown Imperial

Suggestions for Piano Music

Beethoven	Adagio from Sonata in C minor (Pathetique)
	First movement from Sonata in C sharp minor (Moonlight)
Chopin	Funeral March
	Prelude in C minor
Debussy	Clair de Lune
Mozart	Elvira Madigan
Tchaikovsky	Chanson Triste
Williams	Cavatina

Professional Choir/Recordings on CD

Bach	Blessed Jesu, We Are Here (choral prelude)
	Jesu, Joy of Man's Desiring
Brahms	How Lovely Are Thy Dwellings Fair
Duruflé	Ubi Caritas et Amor, Deus ibi est (Where There Is Charity and Love, There Is God)
Elgar	Ave Verum Corpus
Fauré	From Requiem:
	Requiem Aeternam
	Sanctus
	In Paradisum
	Pie Jesu
	Cantique de Jean Racine
Frank	Panis Angelicus
Handel	Where E'er You Walk
Lloyd Webber	Pie Jesu
Loveland/Graham	You Raise Me Up
Mendelssohn	I Waited For The Lord
Morgan	Count Your Blessings
Mozart	Alleluia
	Ave Verum Corpus
	From Requiem (K626)
	Lacrimosa
	Sanctus
	Laudate Dominum (Vespers K339)
Newton	Amazing Grace
Puccini	Nessun Dorma (from Turandot)
Purcell	Rejoice In The Lord Always
	Funeral Sentences
Rutter	Pie Jesu
	God Be In My Head
	Panis Angelicus
	The Lord Bless You And Keep You (Gaelic/Irish Blessing)
Schubert	The Lord Is My Shepherd
Walford Davies	God Be In My Head

Popular Music on CD

The Beatles	Let It Be
Andrea Bocelli/ Celine Dion	The Prayer
Eric Clapton	Tears In Heaven
Darion/Leigh	The Impossible Dream (from Man of La Mancha)
Celine Dion	Because You Loved Me
	Fly
	My Heart Will Go On
Brian Ferry/ Holt Marvell	These Foolish Things
Howard Goodall	The Lord is My Shepherd (theme from The Vicar of Dibley)
Green Day	Good Riddance (Time Of Your Life)
Elton John	Candle in the Wind
	Song for Guy
Lloyd Webber	Love Changes Everything (from Aspects of Love)
Metallica	Nothing Else Matters
Monty Python	Always Look On The Bright Side of Life
Oasis	Live Forever
Queen	The Show Must Go On
	Who Wants To Live Forever?
REM	Everybody Hurts
Rogers and Hammerstein	Climb Every Mountain (from The Sound of Music) You'll Never Walk Alone (from Carousel)
Simon and Garfunkel	Bridge Over Troubled Water
Frank Sinatra	My Way
Rod Stewart	Sailing
Tina Turner	Simply The Best
U2	With Or Without You
Robbie Williams	Angels
Led Zeppelin	Stairway To Heaven

USEFUL ADDRESSES

Many of these organisations will have regional branches, with telephone numbers listed in your local directory.

AB Welfare and Wildlife Trust
Information on woodland or green burial sites.
7 Knox Rd, Harrogate, North Yorkshire HG1 3EF
01423 530900

Action for Victims of Medical Accidents (AVMA)
44 High Street, Croydon, Surrey CR0 1YB
020 8685 8333
E-mail: admin@avma.org.uk

Age Concern Cymru
4th Floor, 1 Cathedral Road, Cardiff, CF1 9SD
02920 371566
www.accymru.org.uk

Age Concern England
Astral House, 1268 London Road, London SW16 4ER
020 8765 7200
www.ageconcern.org.uk

Age Concern Funeral Plan
Freephone 0800 387718

Age Concern Northern Ireland
3 Lower Crescent, Belfast BT7 1NR
02890 245729
E-mail: info@ageconcernni.org

Age Concern Scotland
113 Rose Street, Edinburgh EH2 3DT
01312 203345
E-mail: enquiries@acsinfo3.freeserve.co.uk

Arka Original Funerals
37 Western Road, Hove, East Sussex BN3 1AF
01273 746011
www.ecopod.co.uk

Ashley Jolly Sudden Adult Death Trust
Support for families who have been bereaved by cardiac arrest.
Anne Jolly, SADS UK,
22 Rowhedge, Brentwood, Essex IG8 0GS
01992 813111
www.sadsuk.org

Asian Funeral Service
209 Kenton Road, Harrow, Middlesex HA3 0HD
020 8909 3737
E-mail: asianfuneralservice@btinternet.com

Association of Burial Authorities
Waterloo House, 155 Upper Street, London N1 1RA
020 7288 2522
www.swa-pr.co.uk

Association of Friendly Societies
4th Floor, 51 Gresham Street, London EC2V 7HQ
020 7216 7436
www.afs.org.uk
E-mail: info@afs.org.uk

Association of Medical Research Charities
61 Gray's Inn Road, London WC1X 8TL
020 7269 8820
www.amrc.org.uk

Association of Natural Burial Grounds
Information on woodland or green burial sites.
Contact through The Natural Death Centre (see below)

Bereavement Register
The Bereavement Register,
Freepost SEA8240, Sevenoaks,
Kent TN13 1YR
0870 600 7222 or 01732 460000
www.the-bereavement-register.org.uk

British Association for Counselling and Psychotherapy (BACP)
BACP House, 35–37 Albert Street,
Rugby, Warwickshire CV21 2SG
0870 443 5252
www.bacp.co.uk

British Association of Cancer United Patients (BACUP)
3 Bath Place, Rivington Street,
London EC2A 3JR
0808 800 1234
www.bacup.org.uk

British Humanist Association
47 Theobald's Road, London
WC1X 8SP
020 7430 0908
www.humanism.org.uk

British Organ Donor Society (BODY)
1 The Rookery, Balsham, Cambridge,
CB1 6DL
01223 893636
www.users.argonet.co.uk/body

Celestis Inc
2444 Times Boulevard, Suite 260,
Houston, Texas TX77005, USA
+1 (713) 522 7282
www.celestis.com

Celtic Caskets
Suppliers of cardboard coffins.
Jona Goldingay, PO Box 279, Hatton,
Derbyshire DE66 5ZR
01283 521194/815999

www.eco.coffins.mcmail.com
E-mail: bio.coffins@mcmail.com

Central Wills Directory
PO Box 28, East Grinstead, West
Sussex RH19 2YY
01342 302602
E-mail: info@willsdirectory.com

Child Bereavement Trust
Aston House, West Wycombe,
Buckinghamshire HP14 3AG
0845 357 1000
www.childbereavement.org.uk

Child Death Helpline
0800 282986
www.childdeathhelpline.org.uk

Citizens Advice Bureau
Find your local office in your
telephone book.
www.citizensadvice.org.uk

Compakta Ltd
2 Newbold Road, Desford,
Leicestershire LE9 5GS
01455 828642

The Compassionate Friends
6 Denmark Street, Bristol, BS1 5DQ
0272 292778
www.compassionatefriends.org

Co-operative Funeralcare
Trafford Plaza, 73 Seymour Grove,
Old Trafford, Manchester, M16 0SG
0800 083 6301
www.co-operativefuneralcare.co.uk

Court of Protection Public Guardianship Office
Archway Tower, 2 Junction Road,
London, N19 5SZ
020 7664 7000
www.guardianship.gov.uk

The Cremation Society of Great Britain
2nd Floor, Brecon House,
16/16a Albion Place, Maidstone,
Kent ME14 5DZ
01622 688292
www.cremation.org.uk

CRUSE Bereavement Care
126 Sheen Road, Richmond, Surrey
TW9 1UR
Office: 020 8939 9530
Helpline: 0870 167 1677
www.crusebereavementcare.org.uk

Department for Work and Pensions
Correspondence Unit, Room 540, The
Adelphi, 1–11 John Adam Street,
London WC2N 6HT
020 7712 2171
www.dwp.gov.uk

DVLA
Swansea SA1 1AA
0870 240 0009
www.open.gov.uk/dvla

Ecopod
See Arka Original Funerals above.

Eternal Ascent
www.eternalascent.com

Eternal Reefs
www.eternalreefs.com

Foreign and Commonwealth Office
Consular Protection and Nationality
and Passport Section, Old Admiralty
Building, Whitehall, London
SW1A 2AF
020 7270 1500

**Foundation for the Study of Infant
Deaths**
Artillery House, 11–19 Artillery Row,
London SW1P 1RT
020 7222 8001
Cot death helpline: 020 7235 1721
www.sids.org.uk/fsid

General Register Office
Family Records Centre,
1 Myddleton Street, London
EC1R 1UW
020 8392 5300
Certificates: 020 7233 9233
www.frc.gov.uk
and
Smedley Hydro, Trafalgar Road,

Birkdale, Merseyside PR8 2HH
01704 569824
Certificates: 01704 550013
www.statistics.gov.uk
E-mail:
certificates.services@ons.gov.uk

General Register Office for Scotland
New Register House, 3 West Register
Street, Edinburgh EH1 3YT
01313 340380
www.open.gov.uk/gros/groshome.htm
E-mail: gros@gtnet.gov.uk

Gillman & Son Funeral Service
Suppliers of cardboard coffins
971 Garratt Lane, Tooting, London
SW17 0LW
020 8672 1557

Grandparents Association
Moot House, The Stow, Harlow,
Essex CM20 3AG
Office: 01279 428040
Helpline: 01279 444964
www.grandparents-association.org.uk

The Green Burial Company PLC
Olney Green Burial Ground, Yardley
Road, Olney, Buckinghamshire
MK46 5EH
01234 241808
www.thegreenburialcompany.plc.uk

Green Endings
141 Fortess Road, Tufnell Park,
London NW5 2HR
020 7424 0345
www.greenendings.co.uk

Green Undertakings of Watchet Ltd
12a Swain Street, Watchet, Somerset
TA23 0AB
01984 632285

Green Undertakings Ltd
Hampden House, Rosliston Road,
Burton-on-Trent, Staffordshire
DE15 9RA
01283 540009
www.greenundertakings.co.uk

Greenfield Coffins Ltd
Ridgwell, Essex CO9 4RU
01440 788866
www.greencoffin.com

Heavens Above Fireworks
01992 578993
www.heavensabovefireworks.com

Help the Aged
Head Office, 207–221 Pentonville
Road, London N1 9UZ
020 7278 1114
www.helptheaged.org.uk

Highsted Farm
Suppliers of Bamboo Eco Coffins.
Highsted Valley, Sittingbourne, Kent
ME9 0AG
01795 472262

HM Inspector of Anatomy
Room 611, Wellington House,
135–5 Waterloo Bridge Road, London
SE1 8UG
020 7972 4551
www.dh.gov.uk
Principal Medical Officer, Room C3.8,
Castle Buildings, Belfast BT4 3SQ

**Home Office Coroners and Burials
Team**
5th Floor, Allington Towers,
19 Allington Street, London
SW1E 5EB
0207 035 5530
Fax: 0207 035 552
www.homeoffice.gov.uk

Hospices UK and Ireland
A list of hospices in the UK and
Ireland plus information.
www.hauraki.co.uk/hospice-uk

If I Should Die
One-stop shop dedicated to practical
information and support.
www.ifishoulddie.co.uk

Inland Revenue
Look in your phone book for your
nearest tax office or Inland Revenue
Enquiry Centre.
www.inlandrevenue.gov.uk

Inquest
Ground Floor, Alexandra National
House, 330 Seven Sisters Road,
London N4 2PJ
020 8802 7430
www.gn.apc.org/inquest

JC Atkinson and Son Ltd
Station Road, Penshaw, Houghton-
Le-Spring, Tyne and Wear DH4 7PE
01913 852599
www.coffins.co.uk

**Jewish Bereavement Counselling
Service**
PO Box 6748, London N3 3BX
020 8349 0839
www.jvisit.org.uk

Joseph A Hey & Son Ltd
Suppliers of cardboard coffins online
or by mail. The cost of a coffin plus
plaque, waterproof lining and pillow
support is approximately £50 plus p&p.
470 Great Horton Road, Bradford,
West Yorkshire BD7 3HR
01274 571021
E-mail: robert@funeralassist.co.uk

The Law Society
113 Chancery Lane, London
WC2A 1PL
0870 606 657
www.lawsociety.org.uk

The Law Society in Wales
Capital Tower, Greyfriars Road,
Cardiff, CF10 3AG
02920 645254
www.lawsociety.org.uk

LegaSEA
www.LegaSEA.com

Lesbian and Gay Bereavement Project
C/o Terence Higgins Trust
Counselling Services, London
Lighthouse, 111–117 Lancaster Road,
London W11 1QT
020 7816 0330
Helpline: 020 7403 5969 (7.30–10.30
pm Tues–Thurs only)

LifeGem
www.LifeGem.com

**Macmillan Cancerline, Macmillan
Cancer Relief**
89 Albert Embankment, London
SE1 7UQ
020 7840 7840
Helpline: 0808 808 2020 (9am–6pm
Mon–Fri)
www.cancerlink.org

Memorials by Artists Ltd
Harriet Frazer MBE or Hilary
Meynell
Snape Priory, Snape, Saxmundham,
Suffolk IP17 1SA
01728 688934
www.memorialsbyartists.co.uk
E-mail:
harriet@memorialsbyartists.co.uk

Miscarriage Association
Clayton Hospital, Northgate,
Wakefield, West Yorkshire WF1 3JS
01924 200799
www.miscarriageassociation.org.uk

**National Association for Pre-paid
Funeral Plans**
618 Warwick Road, Solihull, West
Midlands B91 1AA
01217 111343

**National Association of Bereavement
Services**
2nd Floor, 4 Pinchin Street, London
E1 1SA
Helpline: 020 7709 9090

**National Association of Funeral
Directors**
618 Warwick Road, Solihull, West
Midlands B91 1AA
01217 111343
www.nafd.org.uk

**National Association of Memorial
Masons**
27a Albert Street, Rugby,
Warwickshire CV21 2SG
01788 542264
www.namm.org.uk

National Association of Widows
48 Queen's Road, Coventry,
Warwickshire CV1 3EH
02476 634848
www.nawidows.org.uk

**National Health Service Organ Donor
Registration Service**
PO Box 14, FREEPOST, Patchway,
Bristol BS34 8ZZ
0845 606 0400
www.nhsorgandonor.net

The National Secular Society
25 Red Lion Square, London
WC1R 4RL
020 7404 3126
www.secularism.org.uk

The Natural Burial Centre
0207 7354 3831

Natural Death Centre
A valuable source of information on
eco-friendly funerals, and publishers
of *The New Natural Death Handbook*
(£15.99 plus p&p).
6 Blackstock Mews, Blackstock Road,
Finsbury Park, London N4 2BT
020 7359 8391
www.naturaldeath.org.uk

Office of Fair Trading
Fleetbank House, 2–6 Salisbury
Square, London EC4Y 8JX
020 7211 8000
www.oft.gov.uk

Peace Funerals
Head Office, Gleadless Mount,
Sheffield S12 2LN
Freephone: 0800 093 0505
www.peacefunerals.co.uk/mawdesley.
html

Probate Application Department
York Probate Registry, Castle
Chambers, Clifford Street, York,
YO1 9RG
01904 666 777
www.courtservice.gov.uk

**Probate Department Principal
Registry**
Family Division, First Avenue House,
42–49 High Holborn, London
WC1V 0NP
020 7947 7000
www.courtservice.gov.uk

The Purple Funeral Company
Suppliers of cardboard, bamboo,
wicker and chipboard coffins
15 High Street, Bishop's Castle,
Shropshire SY9 5BE
01588 638444

Quakers – see Society of Friends

Registry of Shipping and Seamen
PO Box 165, Cardiff CF14 5FU
02920 768227
E-mail: rss@mcga.gov.uk

Retained Organs Commission
PO Box 32794, London SE1 6WA
Helpline: 0800 838 909

Road Peace
Supports the victims of road accidents
and their families and has an on-going
campaign to reduce danger on the
roads.
PO Box 2579, London NW10 3PW
020 8838 5102
www.roadpeace.org

The Samaritans
The Upper Mill, Kingston Road,
Ewell, Surrey KT17 2AF
020 8394 8300
Helpline: 08457 909090
www.samaritans.org.uk

Scottish Executive Civil Law Division
St Andrew's House, Edinburgh
EH1 3DG
01312 443581
www.scotland.gov.uk

Sea Fisheries Inspectorate
Area 7 A–D, 3–8 Whitehall Place,
London SW1A 2HH
020 7270 8328
Helpdesk: 0845 933 5577
www.defra.gov.uk

Silent Call Guard
Telephone 0870 444 3969 to register.

**Society of Allied and Independent
Funeral Directors**
Business Centre, 4 Bullfields,
Sawbridgeworth, Hertfordshire
CN21 9BD
01279 726777
www.saiflink.org

Society of Friends
Friends House, 173 Euston Road,
London NW1 2BJ
020 7663 1000
www.quaker.org.uk

SSAFA Forces Help
Supports serving and ex-servicemen
and women and their families in need.
19 Queen Elizabeth Street, London
SE1 2LP
020 7403 8783
www.ssafa.org.uk

**Stillbirth and Neonatal Deaths Society
(SANDS)**
28 Portland Place, London W1B 1LY
020 7436 7940
Helpline: 020 7436 5881 (10am–3pm
Mon–Fri)
www.uk-sands.org

Support after Murder and Manslaughter (SAMM)
Offers support to families bereaved through murder and manslaughter.
Cranmer House, 39 Brixton Road, London SW9 6DZ
020 7735 3838
www.samm.org.uk

Support in Bereavement for Brothers and Sisters (SIBBS)
c/o The Compassionate Friends UK (TFC), 53 North Street, Bristol BS3 1EN
0845 1203 785
Helpline: 0845 1232 304
www.tcf.org.uk

Survivors of Bereavement by Suicide (SOBS)
National Office, Centre 88, Saner Street, Hull, HU3 2TR
01482 610728
Helpline: 0870 3337
www.uk-sobs.org.uk

Telephone Preference Service
To register, telephone or apply online at www.tpsonline.org.uk.

Terence Higgins Trust
For sufferers of HIV/AIDS and those who care for them.
52–54 Gray's Inn Road, London WC1X 8JU
020 7831 0330
Helpline: 0845 122 1200
www.tht.org.uk

UK Funerals On-line
3 Dunfield Road, Bellingham, London SE6 3RQ
www.uk-funerals.co.uk

UK Transplant
Enquiries in writing only.
Information Executive, Foxden Road, Stoke Gifford, Bristol BS34 8RR
www.uktransplant.org.uk

Veterans Agency
Thornton-Cleveleys, Lancashire FY5 3WP
Freephone: 0800 169 2277
(8.15am–5.15pm Mon–Thurs, 8.15am–2.30pm Fri)
www.mod.uk/issues/pensions
E-mail
help@veteransagency.gsi.gov.uk

Victim Support
Cranmer House, 39 Brixton Road, London SW9 6DZ
020 7735 9166
www.victimsupport.org.uk

Voluntary Euthanasia Society
13 Prince of Wales Terrace, London W8 5PG
020 7937 7770
www.ves.org.uk

War Pensions Agency
Norcross, Blackpool FY5 3WP
Helpline: 0800 169 2277
www.warpensions.gov.uk

BIBLIOGRAPHY

Bauby, Jean-Dominique. *The Diving Bell and the Butterfly*.
Vintage International.

Baum, Rachel R (ed). *Funeral and Memorial Service Readings,
Poems and Tributes*. McFarland & Company Inc.

Bentley, James, Best, Andrew & Hunt, Jackie. *Funerals: A
Guide*. Hodder and Stoughton Ltd.

Castle, Fiona. *Rainbows Through the Rain*. Hodder &
Stoughton.

Cotter, Jim. *Prayer in the Morning*. Cairns Publishing.

de la Noy, Michael. *The Fields of Praise*. Religious Education
Press Ltd.

Dominica, Sister Frances. *Just My Reflection*. Darton, Longman
and Todd Ltd.

Evans, Nicholas. *The Smoke Jumper*. Dell Publishing.

Gibran, Kahlil. *The Prophet*. Jonathan Cape.

McAinsh, Beverley. *Something Understood*, Hodder Headline.

Munro, Eleanor. *Readings for Remembrance*. Penguin.

Pagett, Andrew (ed). *English Poetry: An Anthology*. Chaucer
Press.

Pryce, Mark (ed). *Literary Companion to the Lectionary*. Society
for Promoting Christian Knowledge.

Rainbows Through Clouds. Published by Lady Glover 1997 for
the Rainbow Trust Children's Charity, Claire House,
Bridge Street, Leatherhead, Surrey KT22 8BZ, Tel: 01372
363438.

Watson, Jean. *Inside Stories: Tales of Change and Growth*. Lion
Publishing plc.

Wavell, A.P. *Other Men's Flowers*. Jonathan Cape.

Whitaker, Agnes (ed). *All in the End is Harvest*. Darton,
Longman and Todd Ltd.

Worthington, Julian. *Making a Will*. W. Foulsham & Co. Ltd.

Wynburne, Rev. John & Gibbs, Alison. *Wedding Readings and
Musical Ideas*. W. Foulsham & Co. Ltd

ACKNOWLEDGEMENTS

'And Death Shall Have No Dominion' by Dylan Thomas from *The Collected Poems by Dylan Thomas*. Reprinted with permission by David Higham Associates Ltd, London

'And Death Shall Have No Dominion' by Dylan Thomas from *The Poems of Dylan Thomas*, Copyright © 1943 by New Directions Publishing Corp. Reprinted by permission of New Directions Publishing Corp.

'Do Not Go Gentle into That Good Night' by Dylan Thomas from *The Collected Poems by Dylan Thomas*. Reprinted with permission by David Higham Associates Ltd, London

'Do Not Go Gentle into That Good Night' by Dylan Thomas from *The Poems of Dylan Thomas*, Copyright © 1952 by Dylan Thomas. Reprinted by permission of New Directions Publishing Corp.

Extract from *Gitanjali* by Rabindranath Tagore. Reprinted by permission of Visva-Bharati University

'Farewell My Friends' by Rabindranath Tagore. Reprinted by permission of Visva-Bharati University

'For These Once Mine' by George Santayana from *The Complete Poems of George Santayana*. Reprinted by permission of Associated University Presses, 2010 Eastpark Boulevard, Cranbury, New Jersey, 08512, USA

'Four Feet' by Rudyard Kipling. Reprinted by permission of A.P. Watt Ltd on behalf of The National Trust for Places of Historic Interest and National Beauty

From 'Modern Man Facing Death' by Metropolitan Anthony of Sourozh. Copyright Cruse Bereavement Care. Extract from a speech made at the Cruse International Conference on Bereavement Following Violence, 1983, summarised in *Bereavement Care*, Winter 1983. Reproduced with permission

'He Wishes for the Cloths of Heaven' by W.B.Yeats. Reprinted from *The Collected Poems of W.B.Yeats* by permission of A.P.Watt Ltd on behalf of Michael B Yeats

'I Have Got My Leave' by Rabindranath Tagore. Reprinted by permission of Visva-Bharati University

'If' by Rudyard Kipling. Reprinted by permission of A.P. Watt Ltd on behalf of The National Trust for Places of Historic Interest and National Beauty

"If I Should Go Before the Rest of You' by Joyce Grenfell (Copyright © The Joyce Grenfell Memorial Trust, 1980) is reproduced by permission of Sheil Land Associates Ltd on behalf of The Estate of Joyce Grenfell

'Letter to a Younger Son' by Christopher Leach. Reprinted by permission of J.M.Dent, a division of The Orion Publishing Group Ltd

'Loss' by Joy Cowley from *Psalms Down Under*. Reprinted with the permission of Joy Cowley, © 'Pieroma', Higginson Street, Otane, 4170, Central Hawkes Bay, New Zealand

'Man Is Spiritual Here and Now' by Joyce Grenfell (Copyright © The Joyce Grenfell Memorial Trust, 1980) is reproduced by permission of Sheil Land Associates Ltd on behalf of The Estate of Joyce Grenfell

'Sea Fever' by John Masefield. Reprinted by permission of The Society of Authors as the Literary Representative of the Estate of John Masefield

'The Bonds of Love' by Dietrich Bonhoeffer from *Letters and Papers from Prison*, the enlarged edition, SCM Press 1971, page 176. Reprinted by permission of SCM Press

'The Glory of the Garden' by Rudyard Kipling. Reprinted by permission of A.P. Watt Ltd on behalf of The National Trust for Places of Historic Interest and National Beauty

'The Old Pattern and the New' by Dr. Colin Murray Parkes. Copyright Cruse Bereavement Care. From: Whitaker, A (ed.) (1984). *All in the End is Harvest: An anthology for those who grieve*. London: Darton, Longman & Todd, p.97

'When I Have Fears' by Noël Coward from *Collected Verse*. © The Estate of Noël Coward. Reprinted by permission of Methuen Publishing Limited

'When You Are Old' by W.B.Yeats. Reprinted from *The Collected Poems of W.B.Yeats* by permission of A.P.Watt Ltd on behalf of Michael B Yeats

'Where Mind Is Without Fear' by Rabindranath Tagore. Reprinted by permission of Visva-Bharati University

INDEX OF FIRST LINES, TITLES AND AUTHORS

INDEX